SEVENTEENTH CENTURY SPANISH MAIN

ATLANTIC OCEAN

Tortuga

Port-de-Paix

HISPAÑOLA

Leoganc

Santo Domingo

Petit Goave

San Juan

PUERTO RICO

St. Eustatius

St. Kitts

San Martin

Nevis

Monserrat

Guadalupe

Antigua

CARIBBEAN SEA

Martinique

Barbados

Curacao

Rio de la Hacha

Margarita

Santa Marta

Coro

Maracaibo

Caracas

Puerto Cabello

Cumana

Trinidad

TERRA FIRMA

✕ Significant Battles & Skirmishes

1666 L'Ollonais brutally attacks **Maracaibo**.

1668 Morgan sacks **Portobello**

1668 Captain Robert Searle sacks **St. Augustine**

1668 L'Ollonais captures **Puerto Caballos**

1668 L'Ollonais is killed on the **Mosquito Coast** by Native Americans.

1669 Morgan sacks **Maracaibo**

1669 Morgan defeats and escapes a Spanish fleet **on Maracaibo Bay**

1670 Rivero de Pardal raids the **Jamaican Coast**

1670 Rivero de Pardal defeats Barnard Speidryke at sea on **Manzanillo Bay**

1670 Rivero de Pardal meets his end off the **South Eastern coast of Cuba** at the hands of English Buccaneers.

1671 Morgan crosses the isthmus of **Panama** and sacks Panama City

Rule Book

Contents

Blood & Plunder

Credits

ORIGINAL DESIGN:
Mike Tuñez

RULEBOOK AUTHOR:
Fred Barnard

PRODUCER:
Alex Aguila

HISTORICAL WRITERS & CONSULTANTS:
Benerson Little
Christopher Tuñez

ILLUSTRATONS & ART DIRECTION:
Ian Hosfeld

PHOTOGRAPHY:
Roberto Ojeda

SCULPTERS:
Brian Rundlett
Jesus Cuevas

GAME COMPONENTS & GRAPHIC DESIGN:
Lilian Figueroa Piedra

STUDIO PAINTER:
Nikolas Obrenović

EDITORS:
Neil Amswych
Melaina Balbo Phipps

OTHER PAINTERS:
Matthew Aravena
Marvin Crone
Chris Kosanke
Jay Pierson

DESIGN CONTRIBUTORS:
Alex Aguila
Robert Alfaro
Jordon Brutlag
Kevin McKay
Joel Sanchez
Steven Soler
Christopher Tuñez

PLAY TESTERS & PROOF READERS:
Neil Amswych
Riley Blair
Duane Boyd
John Burkwall
Joseph Dieguez
Jonathan Dispigno
Henry Durand
Gabriel Garcia
Jack Jackson
Sean Martin
Oscar Morejón
Steven Murga
Dave Olsen
Tom Pace
Hector Penton
Tim Rudy
Tracy Tompkins
Nathan Williams

OTHER CONTRIBUTORS:
Lou Oh
Rune Hoff Lauridsen

I
Historical Overview

rom the piratical free-for-all following the conquest of Spanish Jamaica, to the turning of the tide against the Spanish-hunting Caribbean sea rovers, Firelock Games brings you the romance and reality of buccaneering combat at sea and ashore!

The game period begins in 1660 as the English conquerors of Jamaica have allied with French filibustiers and *boucaniers* from Tortuga, and sent small vessels far and wide to raid Spanish ships and towns along the Spanish Main. Using their skills in intelligence collection, maritime combat, and land warfare, these rovers struck greedy blows against New World Spain.

Yet not for the purpose of rebellion do these men engage their enemy with musket and cutlass, for these rovers are rebels only in the sense that all adventurers are rebels. Nor for patriotism do these men engage their enemy, except in the narrowest sense.

They are motivated foremost by **Blood & Plunder**.

The former the means, the latter the end!

But this period is not so simple as pirate versus Spaniard, or pirate versus pirate hunter. The various players and their individual nationalities, ethnicities, social classes, and physical environments—not to mention their motivations, martial abilities, and loyalties vary greatly and will make or break history.

In fact, if there is any single characteristic of this era, it is diversity: of peoples, geography, vessels, arms, units, tactics, and scale. It is men against each other and simultaneously against the environment. It is English brigantine versus Spanish frigate, buccaneer raider versus Spanish town, *guarda costa* versus interloping smuggler or logwood cutter. It is pirates successfully attacking a mere palisaded fort, it is a pirate ship shattered by a powerful castle. It is Spanish militia defending home and property, it is African slaves fighting to protect their Maroon colony or to escape servitude, it is Native Americans fighting one or all to preserve their way of life.

Among the buccaneers and filibusters are men of many nations, races, ethnicities, and tongues. In fact, some of the most famous "French" filibusters are Dutch, notwithstanding that the Dutch in the Caribbean prefer to trade with Spain, rather than attack her. Likewise, among the Spanish *guardas costas* are not only native Spanish, both *criollos* and *peninsulares*, but also Africans, Native Americans, American born mulattos and meztizos, plus English, French, Dutch, Portuguese, Italians, Corsicans, Greeks and other Levanters, and many others.

Similarly, Spanish militias are not entirely composed of white Spaniards dressed like the sixteenth–century conquistadors we see in pirate films, but are a variety of races and ethnicities, and range from small numbers of professional Spanish soldiers to much larger numbers of conventional militia, lanceros wielding lance and machete, and Native Americans wielding bow and arrow.

For Native Americans, the period is the beginning of the end. Some are under Spanish subjugation, some remain fiercely independent, and sadly some tribes are no more. Some independent Native Americans will ally with Spanish enemies, some with the Spanish themselves.

Most Africans are slaves. A small number are free, and of these some are members of buccaneer crews, others of Spanish militias and pirate hunter crews, and still others of Maroon colonies. A few will become free—or die—leading slave rebellions. Nonetheless, most remain treated as slaves by all sides, even free men of color when captured by the enemy.

The history of the period itself is just as diverse. Beginning with the lawful encouragement of buccaneers and filibusters as a means of defending and financing English and French colonies, we see a slow descent into quasi-piracy and even occasional outright piracy, with accompanying Spanish reprisals, which lead in turn to English and French reprisals . . . and on and on.

After peace is established with Spain in the aftermath of Henry Morgan's sack of Panama in 1671, local governors begin issuing dubious privateering commissions, and even unlawful ones. Merchants continue to greedily trade for pirate goods, openly if they can, in secret if necessary.

Buccaneer and filibuster attacks on Spanish ship and shore continue. Although the attacks are not always successful, they far more often than not are, and this success becomes part of the undoing of English buccaneers, and later the French filibusters. Both have become a threat to trade and peace with Spain, and there is a fear that they might retaliate against English and French colonies and shipping if they are not allowed to continue their attacks on Spanish ships and towns. Yet each time war or politics intervene in this period, Caribbean governors rush to recruit their buccaneers and filibusters as privateers.

Even so, England, and France more slowly, begin to suppress these sea thieves, leading many, beginning in 1680, to cross the Isthmus of Darien or sail around Cape Horn and raid the Spanish in the South Sea, as the Pacific was then known.

Pirate hunters are several times successful, and some buccaneers and filibusters become acquainted with a hempen noose or garrote. Only the advent of war in the closing years of the 1680s saves the buccaneer and filibustier, at least for a while.

Put simply, given that it reflects the reality of the time, the game can be as simple or complex as you desire!

I.1 *Buccaneers and Filibusters: A Chronology*
A FEW BACKGROUND EVENTS

1630 The first *boucaniers*—*chasseurs* or hunters of cattle and swine—appear on Saint-Domingue (western Hispaniola) prior to this year.

English settlers fleeing from Nevis reinforce Tortuga.

The Providence Company of England claims and colonizes [Old] Providence Island (Santa Catalina) and San Andreas Island.

1631 The Providence Company claims Tortuga on the north coast of Saint-Domingue, Hispaniola. Bermudians and other West Indian English settle on the island.

1633 English privateers bring two Spanish prizes into Tortuga.

1633 – 1639 Diego, also called Diegalitto and Diego the Mulatto, raids the Caribbean under a Dutch commission, often in company with Cornelis Corneliszoon Jol, also known as Pie de Palo or Wooden Leg. This is a period of extensive Dutch privateering and naval operations against the Spanish in the Caribbean.

1634 The French *corsaires* of the Antilles begin to be called flibustiers from the English freebooter, from the Dutch *vrijbuiter*.

John Murphy, an Irishman, commits murder in Tortuga and flees to the Spanish. Years later he will help defend Vera Cruz against Laurens de Graaf.

Capt. Petit cruises from Saint-Domingue in Le Ruze.

1635 English settlers defeat a Spanish attack at [Old] Providence Island. Around this time Willem Blauvelt and his father raid the Spanish, using the island as a base.

1637 – 1641 Tortuga flibustiers attack Spanish vessels sailing from Puerto Rico.

1638 The Spanish attack the Dutch at Isla de Tortuga off Venezuela and dislodge them.

1639 Dutch freebooters are active on the Spanish Main, often visiting Providence Island.

1640 Tortuga becomes the central point for the exportation of boucaned meat and hides from the boucaniers of San Domingue. *Boucaniers* begin settling along the north coast of Saint-Domingue.

English settlers at Providence repulse a Spanish raid of 12 vessels and 600 men.

1642 – 1650 The English Civil War is fought over a disagreement between Parliament and the Crown, between Puritans and Royalists. It's aftermath will determine the course of privateering and piracy in the Caribbean.

1640 – 1668 Portugal is at war with Spain. The war serves as a pretext for the issuing of Portuguese commissions for buccaneers and flibustiers when England and Spain, and France and Spain, are at peace.

1640 – 1654 Numerous raids along the coasts of Campeche and Cuba bring Native American and African Americans as slaves to Tortuga. Many will eventually join the boucaniers and flibustiers of San Domingue.

1641 Spain recaptures [Old] Providence Island, their Treasure Fleet overwhelming the colonists.

1648 Capt. Martin operates out of Tortuga, and continues to do so until at least 1661.

1649 Capt. Blauvelt (aka Blewfield) brings a Spanish prize into Rhode Island, then New Amsterdam, captured on the Tabasco river.

1652 In January, flibustiers operating from Tortuga sack Barbacoa, Cuba.

Nearly 500 *boucaniers* now reside at San Domingue in twenty-seven places in groups of ten to fifty, especially on the north and west coasts. On Tortuga are four to five hundred Europeans, of whom fifty or so are English or Irish. From this point forward, two or three Dutch ships per year will come to trade at Tortuga.

Governor Levasseur of Tortuga, a Huguenot gentleman, is assassinated. Levasseur had been intent on setting himself up as an independent prince on the island. M. de Poincy intends to retake control of the island from the rebels, and assigns the Chevalier de Fontenay for this task. Under Fontenay, Tortuga flibustiers make numerous raids not only for hides, meat, and fruit, but they also pillage *"les estancias et les barques de commerce."*

During the summer, Prince Rupert, nephew of the beheaded Charles I of England, cruises the Caribbean.

In August, Tortuga flibustiers sack San Juan de los Remedios del Cayo, Cuba. Flibustiers are actively raiding the Spanish in the Caribbean.

Capt. Martin raids for slaves on the Campeche coast.

1653 Capt. Thomas Harding captures a Dutch vessel in a Barbadian harbor, claiming it is trading with the Spanish. He is tried for piracy in Boston.

At least seven flibustiers are now operating out of Tortuga: two English, two French, two Flemish, and one mulatto privateer named Diego.

1654 The Spanish recapture Tortuga. The Dutch capture Tobago from the Spanish.

In April, Carib Indians (Kalinago) and French colonists in the Antilles exchange blows.

In August, a flibustier attempt to recapture Tortuga fails.

THE PERIOD OF BLOOD & PLUNDER!

1655 In April, an English expedition to seize Santo Domingo from the Spanish, part of Oliver Cromwell's Western Design, fails miserably.

In May, the English expedition, having failed at Santo Domingo, captures Jamaica in a consolation victory. The remaining Spanish engage in a guerrilla war in the mountains

Two Spanish *Galeones de Azogues* (mercury or "quicksilver" galleons), of the *Azogues de Nueva España*, and a patache arrive in Veracruz in May and depart in June.

Two more *Galeones de Azogues* arrive in Veracruz in August and depart a month later.

The first English "buccaneering" raid—if the seizure of Jamaica is not counted—takes place: English naval and ground forces sack Santa Marta in August. The first of those soon to be known as "buccaneers" accompany the naval force.

In August, Spanish settlers are ordered by the Spanish governor to evacuate Tortuga. English and French adventurers quickly reoccupy the island.

England declares war on Spain in October.

The *Flota de Tierra Firma* departs Spain and arrives at Portobello. It is attacked near Cadiz upon its return to Spain.

1656 Admiral William Goodson is appointed head of the Jamaica naval station. Edward D'Oyley becomes Governor of Jamaica and issues letters of marque against Spain. French flibustiers come to Jamaica to accept commissions against the Spanish.

In May, English forces operating out of Jamaica attack Rió de la Hacha. Over the summer, the force, commanded by Admiral Goodson, seeks but misses the Spanish treasure fleet, and briefly blockades Havana.

The French begin resettling Tortuga.

The *Flota de Nueva España* arrives in Veracruz in June and departs in August. It is attacked by an English naval force under Admiral Blake at Tenerife upon its return in 1657: two galleons, eight merchantmen, and a patache are burned.

1657 Admiral Goodson returns to England.

Du Rausset commissions Tortuga flibustiers to attack the Spanish.

In October, Carib Indians (Kalinago) and the French in the Antilles agree to peace.

1658 Capt. de Fontenay attempts to sail to the South Sea to raid the Spanish, but is turned back by weather in January.

In February, Goodson's replacement, Capt. Christopher Myngs, arrives in Jamaica. He organizes Jamaican coastal defenses and captures numerous Dutch vessels for trading with the Spanish, although a prize court will only award one of them as good prize.

In May, Spain lands 550 New Spain soldiers on Jamaica. Myngs seeks reinforcements, lands his own troops, and after a bloody battle defeats the Spanish.

As a reprisal, in the summer Capt. Myngs attacks Santa Marta and Tolu, capturing three vessels. He sells the captured vessels to the buccaneers Searles (Cagway), Prins (Pearl), and Morris (Dolphin).

In September, the French in the Antilles make devastating attacks upon local Caribs (Kalinago).

The English at Jamaica recruit French boucaniers to help hunt renegade Spaniards in the mountains.

The *Flota de Nueva España* arrives at Veracruz, and returns to Spain the following year.

The *Armada de Tierra Firma*, composed of twelve treasure ships, including two men-of-war of the Spanish sails to Portobello and returns to Spain. Four ships are lost during the voyage.

1659 In January, Capt. Myngs continues his strategy of fast sudden attacks in areas far removed from his last attacks. With buccaneer support, he sacks Cumana, Puerto Caballo, and Coro. He is afterward accused of plundering captured treasure, and is arrested and sent to England.

In April, English buccaneers and French flibustiers, operating from Tortuga, plunder Santiago de los Caballeros, Cuba.

Jérémie Deschamps du Rausset is appointed Governor of Tortuga. He organizes defenses, consolidates the colony, and sets the stage for the soon-to-be flibustier and buccaneer stronghold. Although Tortuga is now the primary French flibustier base, du Rausset will soon set his own headquarters at Petit Goave, Saint-Domingue.

Buccaneer or flibustier captains Laques, Gregge, Bonnidell, Bequell, Peterson, Pain (Lepene), Guy, and Williams (aka Willem, Yanky) are commissioned in Port Royal. Yanky and Pain purchase Spanish prizes and rename them Jamaica and Bonaventure. The governor of Jamaica permits Williams to recruit from the HMS Marston Moor, adding

English naval seamen to the buccaneer pool.

Capt. Peterson captures a Dutch slaver and is branded a pirate.

Peace is made between England and Spain, although there is "No peace beyond the line"—in the Americas, that is.

1660 Jean-David Nau, later known as l'Olonnais, arrives in the Antilles as an *engagé* (indentured servant).

In March, Carib Indians (Kalinago) sign a treaty of peace with the French.

The Royal Company of English Commerce with Africa—a slavery corporation—is founded by the Duke of York.

Buccaneer captains Mansfield, Allen, Risby, Wade, and James are commissioned at Port Royal.

Spanish guerrillas are finally defeated, or are otherwise forced from Jamaica.

The Spanish recapture [Old] Providence Island from English buccaneers.

The *Flota de Nueva España* arrives in Veracruz in May, and departs for Spain the following year.

The *Armada de Tierra Firma* departs Spain in September for Portobello, and returns to Spain the following year.

1661 In a policy change, England will try to trade with Spanish colonies, not attack them.

Capt. Wilkes, commanding the HMS Convertine, is ordered to capture the buccaneers Martyn (Martin), Foxery, Taylor, Medlicoate, and Freeborne on charges of piracy.

1662 A small English expedition attempts to capture Tortuga from the French, but fails. The attackers are soon afterward captured by the Spanish.

In July, Capt. Myngs returns to the Caribbean aboard the HMS Centurion, with the HMS Griffin as consort. Governor Windsor of Jamaica is aboard, and will use the likely Spanish refusal of trade as a pretext to attack Spanish ships and towns.

In September, after the Spanish have refused to cooperate, and Lord Windsor issues letters of marque to buccaneers.

In October, Capt. Myngs leads an expedition against Santiago de Cuba, sacking it and destroying its castle. His force is comprised of fifteen hundred men. One thousand of them are buccaneers, among them is Henry Morgan.

In December, the Jamaica Council authorizes more raids against the Spanish. Lord Windsor has returned to England.

Capt. Douglas, operating under a Portuguese commission from Lisbon, captures a Dutch vessel in Jamaica and accuses its captain of having a Jewish merchant aboard to facilitate trading with the Spanish. He sails to Massachusetts where the vessel is impounded on charges of having been illegally seized.

The *Flota de Nueva España* sails from Spain for Veracruz in July, and returns to Spain the following year.

The *Armada de Tierra Firma* departs Spain in November for Portobello, and returns to Spain the following year.

1663 In January, the English from Jamaica try but fail to lure the flibustiers and boucaniers at Tortuga over to English rule.

Capt. Myngs, along with Captains Smart, Mansfield, and James, raid Campeche in February. Myngs is wounded. Capt. Mansfield takes command and finishes the battle. Afterward, Myngs returns to England and is knighted.

During this year, Capt. Blewfields (Blauvelt) sails a barque of fifty men (Dutch, English, and Indian) and three guns out of Blewfields on the Moskito Coast, named for him or his father, still so-named today.

Captains David, Herdue, Clostree are commissioned out of Tortuga. Captains Cooper, Senolve, Smart, Whetstone, Moreau are commissioned out of Port Royal.

The Spanish *Assiento de Negros* (slave trade monopoly) is granted to Domenico Grillo and Ambrosio Lomelin from Genoa, Italy.

At one point this year, Jamaica has one thousand active buccaneers and twelve buccaneer vessels. Tortuga has 258 active flibustiers and four ships (a flute of the governor, and three flibustier vessels, two of them commanded by Frenchman, the third by a Dutchman).

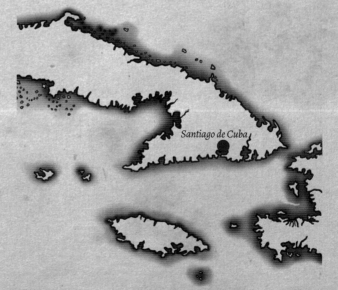

Santiago de Cuba

1664 In May, Edward Morgan arrives as lieutenant governor of Jamaica.

In June, a combined English and Carib (Kalinago) expedition originating from Barbados dislodges the French from Saint-Lucia.

Also in June, the new governor of Jamaica, Thomas Modyford, arrives at Jamaica and declares that hostilities against Spain shall cease. He revokes all privateering commissions. Buccaneers begin to set sail for Tortuga, including many English, Irish, and Dutch.

In September, Capt. Robert Searles arrives in Jamaica with two Spanish prizes. Governor Modyford has them seized and restored to Spain.

Likewise, Williams petitions to bring in a prize, is refused, brings the prize in anyway, and the governor has it seized. The Crown reiterates its non-aggression policy toward Spain, but soon Modyford, requiring buccaneers for the colony's defense, begins turning a blind eye to much of the buccaneering.

In November, Governor du Rausset of Tortuga, now inhabiting the Bastille in Paris, France, for offering the island to England, sells the island to the *Compagnie des Indes Occidentales*. The Compagnie appoints Bertrand d'Ogeron governor.

England begins sending some death-sentenced criminals to the colonies instead of hanging them, adding to the pool of buccaneer recruits.

The *Armada de Tierra Firma* departs Spain for Portobello, and returns to Spain the following year.

Spanish *Azogues de Nueva España* sail to Veracruz and return the following year.

1665 The Second Anglo-Dutch War begins. England lifts prohibitions on attacks against the Dutch.

In February, Captains Morgan, Freeman, Kackman, Morris, and Martien sack Villahermosa de Tabasco, after seizing a Spanish frigate in Campeche Bay.

Governor Modyford, anticipating war with the Dutch, assigns Colonel Edward Morgan (Henry Morgan's uncle) to attack the Dutch in the Caribbean.

Captains Prins and Searle attack the Dutch island of Bonaire.

In March, Capt. Morgan and his raiders defeat a Spanish force sent against them.

In April, famous Dutch admiral de Ruyter arrives in the Caribbean with his fleet.

Captains Morris, Martien, Morgan, and others sack Granada in June.

In July, Governor Morgan leads a mixed rabble of buccaneers, flibustiers, and convicts against the Dutch at Saint Eustace, Saba, Martin, and Tortola, then against the Cuban town of Santa Espiritu instead of Curaçao. After numerous near mutinies and the death of Edward Morgan, Capt. Mansfield becomes the men's principal representative and commander.

At Boca del Toro the raiders split into two groups.

English Bermudan privateer John Wentworth captures Tortola from the Dutch in July.

Governor Modyford recruits English buccaneers to attack the Dutch, in spite of the buccaneers' preference for attacking the Spanish with whom England is now at peace.

In November, buccaneers sack several Cuban towns, claiming this is justified by Portuguese commissions issued by the French governor at Tortuga.

Also this year, Governor Modyford tries and convicts fourteen buccaneers for piracy, but all but three are acquitted. Those found guilty are hanged.

The *Flota de Nueva España* departs Spain for Veracruz and returns the following year.

1666 In January, Captains Searles and Stedman sack the Dutch island of Tobago.

France declares war on England.

In March, Governor Modyford, needing to pacify the buccaneers in order to keep them for the defense of Jamaica, issues privateering commissions against the Spanish. All comers are welcome.

In April, Capt. Mansfield's buccaneers attack Portete and Matina in Costa Rica, but failing to take Cartago, are defeated by jungle and militia.

The English and French at St. Kitts fight for control of the island. The French win. Other conflicts break out between the French and English in the Antilles.

l'Olonnais brutally sacks Maracaibo and Gibraltar.

In May, Mansfield heads to [Old] Providence and recaptures it from the Spanish, intending it as an English (or independent) "Providence" near the Main.

The *Flota de Nueva España* departs Spain in May for Veracruz and returns the following year.

In August, the Spanish recapture [Old] Providence.

In September, the French capture Tobago from the English via a simple ruse.

The French capture Antigua from the English in November.

Also this year, Alexandre Exquemelin arrives at Tortuga as part of the two thousand *engagés* brought there between 1665 and 1667 to support the colony. Women are brought to Tortuga as potential brides.

1667 In February, French forces capture Montserrat. Dutch commander Abraham Crijnssen recaptures Suri-

name from the English.

In May, a combined Franco-Dutch fleet engages an English fleet near Nevis.

France declares war on Spain in May.

In July, the Second Anglo-Dutch War comes to an end: peace reigns again between England and the Netherlands.

In August, l'Olonnais captures a Spanish force sent against him.

The new *Armada de Barlovento*—the Windward Fleet intended to defend the Spanish Caribbean against enemy and pirate attacks, and to defend the treasure fleets in the Caribbean—arrives at Veracruz in September, escorting the *Azogues de Nueva España*. The core of the Armada are four Dutch-built warships.

In October, the English recapture Suriname from the Dutch, but the peace treaty requires the colony remain in Dutch possession.

Also this year, the English Company of Royal Adventurers of Africa, a slave trading corporation, goes bankrupt.

Governor d'Ogeron of Tortuga sends M. Delisle with a force of flibustiers and *boucaniers* to attack Santiago de los Caballeros in reprisal for attacks on the island of Saint-Domingue.

The *Armada de Tierra Firme* arrives at Portobello.

1668 The majority of the *Armada de Barlovento* sails for Spain in January, escorting the *Armada de Tierra Firma*.

In February, war ends between Spain and Portugal.

Buccaneers sack San Juan de los Remedios in Cuba.

In March and April, Capt. Henry Morgan and his buccaneers and flibustiers sack Puerto Principe. Afterward, he sails to Cape Gracios a Dios, but many of his followers part company, unhappy with the plunder from Puerto Principe and with his plan to attack Portobello.

In the spring, l'Olonnais has his last adventures: he captures Puerto Caballos, attempts a raid inland but is repulsed, captures the Honduras urca, and is eventually shipwrecked on the Gulf of Darien where he is killed by local Native Americans.

In May, Capt. Searles and his buccaneers sack St. Augustine, Florida. As a result, Spain will spend the next decade replacing the old wooden fort with one of masonry.

In July, Captain Morgan and his buccaneer flotilla sack Portobello, the great port of the Spanish treasure fleet and home of the great trade fair, on the Isthmus of Darien.

In October, Capt. Morgan and many buccaneers rendezvous at Île-à-Vache in preparation for further expeditions against the Spanish.

Also this year, Capt. Demster, an English buccaneer, briefly blockades Havana.

The *Flota de Nueva España* arrives at Veracruz. It will not return to Spain until 1670.

1669 In January, the now much-reduced *Armada de Barlovento* searches for buccaneers and flibustiers, in particular those who sacked Portobello.

At Île-à-Vache, Henry Morgan's flagship, the HMS Oxford, blows up by accident, killing almost everyone aboard. For the most part, only the officers in the great cabin, including Morgan, survive.

In February, a French naval squadron under the command of the Comte d'Estrées arrives in the Caribbean.

In the spring, Captains Bradley, Brasiliano, and Lecat are active along the Mexican Gulf Coast.

In March, Capt. Henry Morgan and his buccaneer flotilla sack Maracaibo and Gibraltar.

In April, Morgan's flotilla finds itself trapped at the mouth of Lake Maracaibo. Morgan delivers a surprise attack against the few remaining ships of the *Armada de Barlovento* and captures or destroys them. Using subterfuge, he soon after escapes by night under the guns of the fort.

In June, Governor Modyford again issues a proclamation against attacks on the Spanish.

In December, Captains Bradley and Brasiliano retreat from Spanish guardas costas sent from Campeche. Brasiliano is soon shipwrecked nearby.

Also this year, the *Armada de Tierra Firme* arrives at Portobello, and returns to Spain the following year.

1670 In January, Capt. Spierdyke is sent by the governor of Jamaica on a conciliatory mission to the Spanish in Cuba (or uses the letter as a subterfuge to trade illegally with the Spanish), but is instead attacked by the Spanish-commissioned Portuguese or Spanish privateer Capt. Manual Rivero Pardal and killed.

In April, English colonists found Charlestown, South Carolina. The colony will soon be a favorite occasional haunt of buccaneers and flibustiers.

In April or May, Capt. Prins uses the excuse of Rivero Pardal to make a reprisal attack on Santa Cruz de Mompox, but is unsuccessful.

In June, Rivero Pardal makes small raids along the Jamaican coast.

In July, Henry Morgan is commissioned to find and destroy Rivero Pardal. Morgan sets sail with a large flotilla.

A Spanish force is sent to dislodge the Charlestown, South Carolina colonists, but retreats without a fight in August.

Also in August, Captains Prins, Harris, and Ludbury sack Granada in Nicaragua.

In September, with the help of a small French naval frigate, Governor d'Ogeron of Tortuga partially suppresses a flibustier rebellion on Saint-Domingue. The flibustiers do not agree with the French West India Company rules regarding trade.

In October, Captains Morris and Rivero Pardal accidentally seek shelter in the same bay. Morris engages and kills Rivero Pardal.

In November, Captain Narborough sails into the South Sea to attempt to force a trade upon the Spanish.

In December, in preparation for an attack on Panama, Henry Morgan captures [Old] Providence Island.

Also this year, Capt. Bradley captures four Spanish vessels at Rancheria while provisioning. One, the Galliandena, goes to Capt. Champagne, then to Capt. Gasconne,.

Gapt. Gasconne is actively operating out of Tortuga.

Petit Goave on Saint-Domingue becomes the central base of operations for flibustiers, and will soon largely replace Tortuga.

The *Flota de Nueva España* arrives at Veracruz and returns to Spain the following year.

1671 In January, Capt. Henry Morgan, with an English commission, captures Chagres, then crosses the Isthmus of Panama and sacks Panama. Capt. Searles and his drunken men miss capturing the Trinidad, and with it much of the wealth and wealthy people of Panama. The attacks have great political repercussions.

In March, Henry Morgan returns to Jamaica and is advised of a new treaty of peace with Spain.

In November, Governor Lynch of Jamaica receives an order to arrest Henry Morgan.

The *Armada Caribe*—seven ships, three frigates, and four chinchorros—is dispatched from Spain in August. Its purpose is to defend Panama and fight pirates.

Also this year, the *Flota de Nueva España* arrives at Veracruz and returns to Spain the following year.

1672 In March, England declares war on the Netherlands.

In March and April, buccaneers or flibustiers burn a *guarda costa* under construction at Campeche, then sack various towns along the Mexican coast.

In June, an English force under Governor Stapleton of the Leeward Islands attacks Dutch colonies in the Antilles and Virgin Islands.

In August, Henry Morgan arrives in England, ostensibly to be tried for crimes.

Also this year, a new *Armada de Barlovento* is formed.

The *Armada de Tierra Firma* arrives at Portobello and returns to Spain the following year.

France and the Netherlands declare war on each other.

1673 Buccaneers raid San Juan de los Remedios, Cuba, in February.

Also in February, Governor d'Ogeran's ship runs aground at Puerto Rico. He and most of his men are captured. D'Ogeron escapes Spanish custody six months later.

In June, Diego the Mulatto (aka Diego Grillo) defeats three Spanish vessels sent to capture him.

In July, Capt. Evertson, a Dutch naval officer, raids the Chesapeake after wreaking havoc in the Caribbean, including the capture of St. Eustace.

In August, buccaneers raid the Mexican coast again. A pirate hunting expedition sets sail from Veracruz, first forcing these buccaneers ashore, then attacks other buccaneers at Laguna de Términos.

In October, Governor d'Ogeron, with five hundred flibustiers, attempts to rescue his imprisoned men on Puerto Rico. The expedition is a debacle, resulting in the release of none and the murder of more than three dozen flibustier prisoners in reprisal.

Also in October, France declares war on Spain. Once again, France will issue legitimate privateering commissions against Spain.

The *Flota de Nueva España* arrives at Veracruz and returns to Spain the following year.

The *Armada de Tierra Firma* arrives at Portobello.

Throughout the year, English and Dutch forces attack each other in the Caribbean, as do French and Dutch forces, and, at year's end, French and Spanish.

1674 The Treaty of Westminster is ratified in March: peace comes again between England and the Netherlands.

In July, Dutch admiral De Ruyter attacks Martinique but is defeated by the French.

In August, Henry Morgan is knighted for his attack on Panama.

Also this year, William Dampier begins work as a plantation overseer in Jamaica.

1675 In the spring, Sir Henry Morgan returns to Jamaica, having first been shipwrecked at Île-à-Vache. Now the lieutenant governor of the island, he counsels patience to buccaneers, and quietly assures them in so many words that their way of life is not at an end.

Governor Vaughn, newly appointed to govern Jamaica, arrives a month after Sir Henry.

Also in the spring, Capt. John Bennet, an Englishman commanding a brigantine with French crew, commission, and colors, captures the *Buen Jesus de las Almas* near Santo Domingo, Hispaniola in April. The small frigate is carrying nearly 50,000 pieces of eight.

In April, English buccaneers are forbidden to serve "foreign princes." Nonetheless, many do, preferring not to give up their sea roving trade.

In August, William Dampier makes his first voyage to Laguna de Términos to trade in logwood. Approximately two hundred and fifty logwood cutters are interloping at Laguna de Términos. Many of them are former buccaneers, or those who are temporarily taking leave of sea roving.

Also this year, the *Armada de Tierra Firma* arrives at Portobello and returns the following year.

The *Flota de Nueva España* arrives at Veracruz and returns to Spain the following year.

Flibustier captains Lessone (La Sound) and the Sieur de Bernanos march into the Isthmus of Darien but are driven back by the Spanish.

Spanish *guardas costas* and privateers are active against buccaneers and flibustiers.

Governor d'Ogeron of Tortuga returns to France, and dies.

Denmark colonizes St. Thomas.

Per treaty, Suriname becomes Dutch, and New York, English.

1676 The Dutch under Admiral Jacob Binkes capture Cayenne from the French in May. Admiral d'Estrées recaptures the island at year's end.

During the spring and summer, Binckes continues to attack French possessions in the New World.

During the summer, Dutch privateers Aernouts and Reyning attack Grenada, but are captured.

In June and July, eight hundred buccaneers under Captains Wright and Lane raid inland into Nicaragua and sack Segovia. They are afterward defeated in Costa Rica. Among their number is Bartholomew Sharp.

In July, Admiral Binckes attacks the outnumbered French at Petit Goave, but receives stout resistance during a naval battle in the harbor. He fails to land troops due to French defenses and reinforcements ashore.

In October, French flibustiers commanded by Capt. LeMoyne capture the Concordia at the Gulf of Honduras. Almost certainly serving aboard the Spanish ship as a Spanish gunner is Dutchman Laurens de Graff, destined to become one of history's greatest flibustiers.

In December, the French under Admiral d'Estrées capture Tobago from the Dutch.

Also this year, Capt. Deane, a buccaneer, is accused of piracy, tried, and acquitted.

Buccaneers, among whose number is William Dampier, sack Alvarado, Mexico, and are almost captured by Spanish armadillas soon after.

1677 In January, the Marquis de Maintenon raids Margarita Island on the coast of Venezuela.

In March, Admiral d'Estrées is defeated in a fleet action by the Dutch off Tobago.

A small flibustier force under Capt. Ribaut attacks Jalapa, Mexico.

In June, flibustiers and buccaneers, including Captains Lagarde, Coxon, and Barnes, sack Santa Marta, capturing the local governor and bishop whom they take to Jamaica in July, intending to hold them for ransom.

In July, two Spanish men-of-war, including the *Francesa*, part of the new *Armada de Barlovento*, arrive at Cartagena and soon seek the buccaneers who attacked Santa Marta, but are chased away. Other ships of the armada arrive at La Guaira, Venezuela, from Cadiz.

In November, Capt. de Franquesnay, a flibustier, lands on the Cuban shore to raid Santiago de Cuba. The raid fails when the attackers get lost.

In December, Admiral d'Estrées, having returned to France after his defeat at Tobago, attacks Tobago again by land and sea, and is victorious.

Also this year, Capt. Browne, a Scotsman, seizes a Dutch trading vessel off Cartagena and sells the slaves illegally in Jamaica, for which he is hanged.

Buccaneers attack San Marcos de Apalache, Florida.

Three flibustier ships, including those commanded by Captains Lemoyne and Bennett, attack the rich Honduras urca. They are resoundingly defeated. The urca is attacked again near Cadiz, this time by Barbary corsairs. Again, the Spanish victory is resounding.

English buccaneers begin returning to Port Royal, Jamaica, after the publication of an Act making it illegal to serve a foreign prince. Among those to accept amnesty are the buccaneers who sacked Santa Marta.

The *Azogues de Nueva España* arrives at Veracruz.

1678 In May, Admiral d'Estrées's fleet runs aground at Aves Island off the Venezuelan coast. Among the shipwrecked are two or three flibustier vessels.

The *Sieur de Grammont* sacks Maracaibo in June, and continues to plunder the region until December.

In July, two hundred buccaneers commanded by Captains Spurre and Neville sack Campeche, Mexico.

In August, peace is made between France and the Netherlands.

In September, peace is made between France and Spain.

Also this year, Capt. LeMoyne, along with Capt. Pérou, captures three Dutch prizes at the Bay of Matanzas in Cuba, under a commission from Governor de Pouancy. Two thirds of the crew are English. LeMoyne takes a fourth prize, or perhaps all of them, to Boston for disposal.

A slave ship wrecks at Capestere, but the crew, and African and Arab slaves, are saved by Carib Indians (Kalinago).

The Earl of Carlisle arrives in Jamaica as governor.

French forces attack Danish St. Thomas but are repulsed.

The *Armada de Tierra Firma* arrives at Portobello and returns the following year.

The *Flota de Nueva España* arrives at Veracruz and returns to Spain the following year.

The first edition of Alexandre Exquemelin's *The Buccaneers of America* is published, in Dutch. This is the first of many editions in several languages.

1679 In February, flibustiers under Capt. Bot land on Cuba, intending to attack Santiago de Cuba, but soon abandon the attempt.

The *Sieur de Grammont* attacks Guanaja, Cuba, but is met with stiff resistance, and must be extricated by Capt. de Graff.

During the summer, *Grammont* cruises the north Cuban coast, hoping to capture prizes heading to or from Havana.

In June, flibustiers under the command of Captains Bot and Bréha attack Spanish treasure salvors at the wreck of the Maravillas.

In August, buccaneers under the command of Capt. Sawkins sack Santa Marta again.

In September, buccaneers under the command of Captains Coxon, Essex, Sharp and probably others capture five hundred chests of indigo and other valuable goods in the Gulf of Honduras.

In December, buccaneers rendezvous at Jamaica for an attack on Portobello.

Also this year, Capt. Edmund Cook seizes a Spanish bark loaded with cacao, in reprisal for the Spanish theft of his trading vessel.

Capt. Cornelius Essex in the *Great Dolphin* plunders the plantation of Major Jenks at St. James Parish in Jamaica. He and his crew are captured. Two are sentenced to hang.

Capt. Peter Harris captures a Dutch ship of 28 guns in the south keys of Cuba.

Capt. Johnson of the Royal Navy captures Capt. Sawkins, the buccaneer. Sawkins is soon released.

Raveneau de Lussan, who will write a book about his adventures as a flibustier, arrives at Saint-Domingue as an *engagé*.

The *Sieur de Grammont* sacks Puerto Principe.

1680 In February, buccaneers under command of Captains Coxon, Sharp, Allison, Essex, Maggott, Sawkins, and others sack Portobello.

Spanish forces capture a few logwood cutters, among whose number are former buccaneers, at Laguna de Térmi-nos. Spanish forces plot a larger attack as soon as possible.

In April, Spanish forces make a large, successful raid against interloping logwood cutters at Laguna de Térmi-nos. Among the Spanish captains are Juan Corso and Pedro de Castro.

A large buccaneer force, whose captains include Sharp, Coxon, Cook, Harris, Allison, and Sawkins, march into the Isthmus of Darien with Native America allies and sack Santa Maria. The buccaneers continue onward to the South Sea (Pacific) coast where they engage and defeat a small force of Spanish armadillas near [New] Panama, then capture a great Spanish ship, which they make their flagship. William Dampier is among these buccaneers.

In June, buccaneers and flibustiers under Captains Grammont, Wright, and Paine sack La Guaira.

In December, the South Sea buccaneers plunder La Serena.

Also this year, the *Flota de Nueva España* arrives at Veracruz and returns to Spain the following year.

The South Sea buccaneers make numerous raids south along the Spanish Pacific coastline.

1681 In February, the South Sea buccaneers, having so far survived low rations, Spanish defenses, and serious disagreements among themselves, are defeated at Arica. Capt. Sharp assumes command and leads a successful retreat.

In May, two great new *Armada de Barlovento*—the *Capitana* and *Almiranta* of the fleet—set sail from Cadiz for Veracruz: both are Dutch-built.

In June, buccaneers raid deeply into Costa Rica.

In November, Capt. Sharp and his buccaneers sail around Cape Horn and return to the Atlantic after raiding the South Sea.

The *Sieur de Grammont* sacks Cumana, but loses all when his ship founders near Petit Goave.

Nicolas Van Horn, soon destined to become a famous flibustier, purchases the *Mary and Martha*, a former hired ship of the English navy, at London, and renames her the *St. Nicolas*.

Also this year, the *Armada de Tierra Firma* arrives at Portobello and returns in 1683. The fleet loses a galleon, three ships, and a patache.

The *Flota de Nueva España* arrives at Veracruz.

Sir Henry Morgan leads militia and volunteers against the pirate Evertson and his crew, and kills or captures them.

Sir Thomas Lynch is appointed Governor of Jamaica.

Carib Indians (Kalinago) attack Antigua and Barbuda.

William Dampier returns to the Caribbean over land via Darien, along with others who have abandoned the South Sea expedition. He will soon sail with Captains Wright and Yanky, who will soon sack Rió de la Hacha.

1682 In February, five filibustier ships, including those commanded by Captains Grammont and de Graff, capture the *Candelaria*, a subsidy ship for St. Augustine, at the upper Florida Keys.

In July, Capt. de Graff captures the *Francesa* from the Spanish, commanded by Manuel Delgado. She is a ship of the *Armada de Barlovento* and is loaded with money and goods for Santo Domingo. The capture causes a financial crisis on the island.

In August, Capt. Foccard, a flibustier sacks Tampico, Mexico.

In November, Spanish authorities seize slaves at Santo Domingo from Capt. Van Horn, in reprisal for pirate attacks. Making his own reprisal, Van Horn turns flibustier, assuming he had not already intended to do so.

Also this year, Capt. Coxon is sent by Lynch to the Bay of Honduras to bring away the English logwood cutters.

Two ships and one hundred flibustiers attack Apalachee, Florida.

Capt. Sharp is arrested in England and tried for piracies against the Spanish in the South Sea. He is acquitted.

1683 Grammont and other captains blockade Cuba, largely unsuccessfully, from late 1682 until early 1683.

In February, Captains Van Horn, dc Graff, and others capture two empty Honduras urcas. Van Horn has ignored de Graff's suggested strategy, beginning a simmering enmity between the two flibustier captains.

In March, Captains Bréha, Markham, Paine, Conway, Wooley, and Cornelis attack St. Augustine, but the city is well defended so they raid the countryside instead.

In May, Spanish privateers from Havana attack Charlestown, South Carolina.

Flibustiers under the command of Grammont, de Graff, and Van Horn brutally sack Veracruz. Near the end of the raid, de Graff and Van Horn have a falling out, and de Graff wounds Van Horn in a duel. Van Horn dies soon afterward.

During the spring and summer, Capt. Cook, a buccaneer, seizes a flibustier vessel in reprisal for an earlier affront, then captures two more vessels and sails to Virginia where he refits and sets sail for the South Sea.

During the summer, Capt. Bot captures the *Nuestra Señora de Regla* after a bloody fight.

In August, the *Armada de Barlovento* captures six flibustier vessels, including Captain Bot's prize.

Capt. Carlisle of the Royal Navy burns the ship of the notorious pirate Hamlin, who attacks ships of all nations, at St. Thomas where he has been hiding out.

In December, Captains Andresson, de Graff, Michel, Yanky, Lesage, and Bréha blockade Cartagena and defeat converted Spanish Assiento (slave) ships sent against them. The flibustiers turn two of them into pirate ships.

Also this year, the *Armada de Tierra Firma* arrives at Portobello.

The *Flota de Nueva España* arrives at Veracruz and returns at the end of the year or the beginning of the next.

Capt. Juan Corso, a Spanish *guarda costa* and pirate, is active, often using Santiago de Cuba as a base.

1684 In January, Spanish privateers sack New Providence Island in the Bahamas in reprisal for the attack on St. Augustine by buccaneers.

In February, Capt. Cook and his buccaneers enter the South Sea via the Strait of Magellan. Other buccaneers will also enter the South Sea this year. Among their number is William Dampier.

In the spring, Spain declares war on France. The war lasts only until August.

In the spring and summer, the *Sieur de Bernanos* and flibustier Captains Grogniet, Blot, Vigneron, and Petit cruise along Brazil and the Gulf of Paria.

In June, Capt. Harris (the nephew) crosses the Isthmus of Darien and by accident links up with other South Sea buccaneers.

In October, buccaneer captains Swan, Harris, and Davis, who linked up the previous month, attack Paita in the South Sea.

Also this year, Capt. de Graff and other flibustiers blockade Cuba. Captains Brouage and Michel capture two Dutch vessels in the service of Spain.

Buccaneer captains Jingle (Yanky?) and Ranson capture the *Plantanera*, a subsidy ship for St. Augustine, at the Keys. Spanish captain Miguel Ramon, sent to seek the pirates, attacks the buccaneers, is defeated, captured, tortured, and set ashore on one of the Keys.

Capt. de Graff and his consorts cruise along the Cuban coast, then to Central America where they link up with Captain Rose. Many flibustiers desert de Graff, preferring to cross over into the South Sea. Among them is Raveneau de Lussan.

Hender Molesworth becomes Governor of Jamaica.

Buccaneers sack Tampico, Mexico.

The *Armada de Tierra Firma* arrives at Portobello and returns to Spain in 1686.

The *Azogues de Nueva España* arrive at Veracruz and return to Spain the following year.

1685 In January, a large party of flibustiers crosses the Isthmus of Darien into the South Sea. De Graff parts company with them.

In April, South Sea flibustiers blockade Panama.

In June, a Spanish naval force engages the South Sea flibustiers. The sea thieves have no choice but to retreat.

In July, Captains Grammont and de Graff lead the sack Campeche. The flibustiers occupy the city for sixty days. Only a few English captains are among the attackers: one of them is Bartholomew Sharp.

In August, the *Armada de Barlovento* sets out in pursuit of the flibustiers who are sacking Campeche.

In September, the *Armada de Barlovento* captures some flibustiers as they sail from Veracruz. Captain Bréha is among the captured. He is hanged at Veracruz.

Also in September, Capt. de Graff, commanding the Neptune, engages the *Capitana* and *Almirante* of the armada in an epic battle, fights them to a draw, and escapes.

Also this year, the pirate Banister makes a daring escape from Port Royal, fired upon by the ports forts as he does. Capt. Dechesne's ship is captured on the coast of Jamaica, but he escapes to join Banister.

Spanish privateers Juan Corso and Pedro de Castro search the Gulf Coast for La Salle's colony, its existence revealed by the interrogation of captured flibustiers.

Capt. Sharp obtains a dubious English commission to pursue "pirates and Indians." Sailing to Bermuda to sell his cargo of slaves captured at Campeche, he helps the local governor put down a rebellion. Soon afterward, he is arrested by Capt. St. Lo of the English Navy and carried to Nevis to be tried for piracy. He will be acquitted of piracy for a second time.

Spanish privateer and pirate Juan Corso sacks New Providence.

1686 South Sea flibustiers and buccaneers continue their raids on the Spanish.

In March and April, Capt. de Graff raids Vallolidad.

In April, South Sea pirates under the command of Captains Grogniet and Townley sack Granada.

In April and May, a scout vessel sent by the *Sieur de Grammont* prior to raiding St. Augustine is shipwrecked at Matanzas on the Florida coast. The scout vessel's crew defends itself for several days before most are captured or killed. The attack on the city is abandoned.

In July, two English men-of-war destroy the pirate Banister's ship while it careens at Samana Bay. Banister escapes with French flibustiers, who later this year head into the South Sea via the Strait of Magellan. Banister, however, parts company with them as soon as he can.

In August, Spanish raiders from St. Augustine destroy the Scottish colony of Port Royal in South Carolina, then plunder the outskirts of Charlestown.

In November, France and England agree to suppress their buccaneers and flibustiers. The heyday of buccaneering is at an end.

The pirate hunting *Vizcayan* squadron arrives in the Caribbean.

Also this year, the *Azogues de Nueva España* arrive at Veracruz, and return to Spain in 1688.

Captain Yanky captures a Spanish ship with a cargo worth fifty thousand pieces of eight.

Captain de Graff's *Neptune* wrecks on a reef near Cartagena.

Captain Swan and his crew cross the Pacific. William Dampier is with them.

Charlestown, South Carolina inhabitants plan a reprisal against St. Augustine, to be joined by flibustiers commanded by the *Sieur de Grammont*, but the new governor quashes the plan.

1687 In February, the pirate Banister is hanged from an English man-of-war in sight of Port Royal, Jamaica.

In March, Governor du Cussy of Saint-Domingue orders all flibustiers to quit attacking the ships and towns of Spain.

In April, South Sea flibustiers sack Guayaquil.

Also this year, the *Azogues de Nueva España* arrive at Veracruz and return to Spain the following year.

The *Flota de Nueva España* arrives at Veracruz and returns to Spain the following year.

The flibustier Le Picard is active in the South Sea.

The pirate hunting *Vizcayan* squadron attacks de Graff but is defeated.

Captain Phips, later to become governor of Massachusetts, recovers great riches from a Spanish wreck on the Abrojos reef.

Spanish privateer Blas Miguel, whose brother was killed in the Vizcayan action against de Graff, sacks Petit Goave, but is forced by a counterattack to retreat into the town's fort, where he and his men are captured, tried, and put to death.

The Duke of Albemarle becomes Governor of Jamaica.

1688 In August, Sir Henry Morgan dies. At his funeral he is given a twenty-two gun salute.

In December, the flibustiers who had consorted with Banister at Samana Bay attack Acaponeta, Mexico, in the South Sea. Their red flag of no quarter is distinctive: upon it is a skull and crossbones, the only known instance of late–seventeenth–century buccaneers and flibustiers flying the symbol.

Also this year, the *Armada de Tierra Firma* arrives at Portobello and returns to Spain the following year.

The *Azogues de Nueva España* arrive at Veracruz and return to Spain the following year.

King James II of England is overthrown in the "Glorious Revolution." Europe prepares for war.

And a Few Teasers for the Next Era ...

1689 Capt. Strong, an English privateer, is commissioned to find a sunken galleon, trade with the Spanish, and attack the French in the South Sea. His voyage is a failure.

Capt. Sharp has gone entirely legitimate, leading a company of buccaneers and volunteers under General Codrington against the French in the Leeward Islands.

1690 The French under M. de Cussy, composed of one thousand men, half habitans, half flibustiers, sack Santiago de los Caballeros.

1691 Capt. Allison seizes an English ship, the *Good Hope*, at Madiera while raking salt.

1692 An earthquake strikes Jamaica, destroying much of Port Royal. However, the earthquake has little to do with the demise of buccaneering, for it has been suppressed for almost a decade.

1698 The Scottish Company sails to Darien to establish a colony, with Capt. Allison as pilot. The Company relies heavily on former buccaneer Lionel Wafer's "secret report."

2
Introduction

lood & Plunder is a skirmish-level tabletop miniatures game that uses 28mm miniatures on 20 mm bases, with ships and battlefield terrain of the same scale. The game is set during the "Golden Age of Piracy" (circa 1660-1680), and depicts the conflicts involving the foreign powers and the indigenous people in the Caribbean during that period.

In Blood & Plunder, two (or more) players use miniatures to represent their soldiers; and build custom forces to represent a warring faction in the Caribbean at that time. A force can consist of just a few miniatures, however owning more miniatures gives a player the option of building larger and more diverse fighting forces.

Firelock Games currently sells a broad selection of miniatures and ships for the factions in Blood & Plunder, and many more will be released as time goes on. All miniatures and ships produced by Firelock Games are supplied unpainted, giving players the option to customize their models in any manner they choose.

To fight a battle, players first build a custom force with the miniatures they have on hand. Players then choose or randomly determine a scenario, which will indicate how opposing forces are set up on the battlefield, and will determine what each player must accomplish to win. For example, a scenario might describe an attempt to capture an enemy commander or to raid an enemy camp for supplies.

Scenarios can take place on land, on ships at sea, or as a combination of both, because Blood & Plunder has a unique set of rules that allows for seamless play between land and sea. The rules are designed to be simple, intuitive, and fun, but still encompass a lot of historical detail.

To give a general overview of the game mechanics, all of the miniatures in a defined group (called a unit) will act at the same time, and that unit will take actions as a group. There are a wide variety of actions a unit may take, such as shooting at an enemy from afar, bringing the fight to a foe in close combat, or trying to shake off the effects of fatigue. The outcomes of many actions are determined by Tests, which involve rolling dice to determine whether a unit has succeeded or failed.

Players have a hand (Activation Cards) that they play to determine which unit may act first, and how many actions that unit may take. Players use these cards in a back-and-forth fashion until all units on the battlefield have taken actions, at which point the turn is over. This process is repeated until the turn limit for the game has elapsed, or a player satisfies their victory conditions.

2.1 *How to Use This book*

In the rules that follow, we will first outline the basics of the game, including the equipment necessary for play, core terminology, and fundamental game mechanics. After that, we will outline activating and taking actions with units. Rounding out the essentials will be a section related to combat. At that point, we suggest you stop reading and enjoy a game of *Blood & Plunder!* You should have enough information to play a land scenario. This will be a good time to get a grasp of the rules before you move on to the ship rules. Skip down to Creating a Force to make a force list, then play the Encounter scenario under Core Scenarios. After that game you should have enough hands-on experience to move on to the rest of the rules with confidence. (If not, keep playing it until you do!)

2.2 *Still Confused? Fear not!*

If you are utterly baffled by the rules you read here, and you think all hope is lost, fear not! There is a series of tutorial videos viewable on Firelock Games YouTube channel. We break down the rules for you step-by-step, with plenty of examples of game play.

In addition, help can always be found in the forums at *www.firelockgames.com*.

FREEBOOTERS
TRAINED — 6

MAIN WEAPON: BUCCANEER GUNS
SIDEARMS: PISTOLS

	SKILL	SAVE	RESOLVE
Fight	6	6	5
Shoot	6	7	

BALL & SHOT* MARKSMEN
FAST RELOAD * SAILORS

GUARDA COSTA CAPTAIN
EXPERIENCED — 15

May Lead Any Guarda Costa Force.

MAIN WEAPON:
PISTOL, STANDARD MELEE WEAPON

COMMAND RANGE 8"

COMMAND POINTS 2

MARINEROS
(Spanish Sailors)
TRAINED — 4

MAIN WEAPON: PISTOLS

	SKILL	SAVE	RESOLVE
Fight	5	7	5
Shoot	7	7	

SAILORS * ARTILLERY CREW
RUTHLESS * POORLY EQUIPPED

3
Game Essentials

3.1 *Dice and Tests*

Blood & Plunder uses 10-sided dice ("d10" for short) to determine the outcome of many situations in the game. A handful (4–12) are required to play.

Rolling the "0" result on a d10 counts as a "10," and is referred to in the rules as a "natural 10." Likewise, a roll of "1" is called a "natural 1".

If the rules refer to rolling a d5, roll a d10 and divide the result in half, rounding up.

If a die is rerolled due to a game mechanic (*e.g., expend a Fortune point*), it may only be rerolled once.

Firelock D10 Dice

Faction D10 Dice (England & Spain)

Figure 1: *ten-sided dice.*

TESTS

Tests are used to determine whether units have failed or succeeded in their attempted actions. They are used in game to determine a variety of outcomes, and each will be detailed fully in the appropriate sections.

All Tests are resolved by rolling a number of d10, applying modifiers if applicable *(See Figure 1)*, and comparing the result of the roll to a target number. The roll must equal or exceed the target number for the Test to be successful.

Sometimes the target number for the Test depends on the skills of a group of miniatures, and sometimes it is a set number. Each Test description will explain how to determine the target number.

For example, a unit of six models needs a 6+ on a Shoot Test to successfully hit another unit. Six d10 are rolled. The results are 1, 2, 6, 8, 10, 10. The shooting unit passed the Shoot Test four times.

MODIFIERS

When performing a Test, certain effects or conditions will make Tests easier or harder to achieve. Bonuses (-X) lower the target number to make Tests easier. Penalties (+X) will force the target number higher to make Tests harder.

For example, a Test that requires a 6 to pass has a +3 penalty. Players can consider the target number of the Test to be 3 higher (9+).

Unless otherwise noted, a Test roll that would require an 11+ is considered impossible and may not be attempted.

3.2 *Measuring Distances*

Although there is a 4" straight ruler built into the ship turning gauge that is useful in many situations, a tape measure will also be necessary to measure the long distances usually involved with Ranged attacks.

All distances in the game are given and measured in inches. Exact measurements in fractions of inches are not important; players will only need to know if a distance is more or less than a whole number *(for example, a distance of 15.75" is considered more than 15" and less than 16")*.

Measurements may be taken at any time for any reason (go ahead and premeasure!—It's fine!), and distances are always measured between the two closest points.

> » When measuring from one unit to another, measure between the bases of the two closest models from each unit.

> » When measuring from a structure, measure from the closest point of a ship's hull or a building's walls, not from an extremity (like the bowsprit of a ship or buttresses on a building).

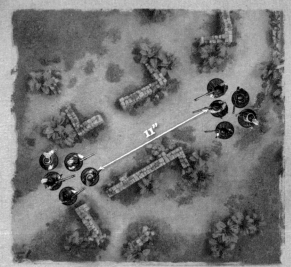

Figure 2

In Figure 2, the closest models in the two units are 11" apart. For the purposes of Ranged Attacks, all models in both units are considered to be 11" apart

3.3 Markers

Markers are necessary to track game effects such as Fatigue, Reload, and Critical damage. Anything can be used as a marker as long as its meaning is clear to both players. Poly-fil "smoke", dice, tokens, etc, are all useful tools for marking various effects.

For your convenience, Firelock Games has produced a range of custom dice markers for Blood & Plunder.

Figure 3: *Fatigue and Reload Markers*

3.4 Activation Cards

A standard deck of playing cards (or the custom decks produced by Firelock Games) will be necessary to play Blood & Plunder. Activation Cards and how to use them are described fully in the next section of the rule book.

Figure 4: *Activation Cards*

3.5 Game Table & Terrain

A flat surface and some terrain pieces of the proper scale are required for play. An area of 3' x 4' is ideal for land and amphibious battles of 200 points or less. A larger play area (up to 4' x 6') is ideal for larger engagements, especially ship battles.

The *Scenarios* section provides more details on laying out a game board of the proper size, while the *Terrain* section explains the effects of terrain on gameplay.

3.6 Sportsmanship!

There may be times during play when players disagree or are unsure how to resolve a situation. Often, this occurs because game rules can be interpreted in different ways.

If this happens, the players in the game should discuss the situation and attempt to come to an agreement. Reaching a consensus between players is more important than getting the rules exactly right. If consensus remains elusive, have a third party make the decision or randomly determine a ruling with a roll of the dice.

Always remember, this is a game about playing detailed and thematic battles in the Golden Age of Piracy! Have fun!

Figure 5: A battlefield with terrain representing a Spanish town

3.7 Miniatures

In order to play, you need miniatures of course! In this section we will lay out the basics for organizing and using your miniatures on the battlefield.

UNIT BASICS

In Blood and Plunder, a single miniature is referred to as a *model*. A group of models of the same type operate together in groups, which are called *units*. All the units (and related miniatures, like ships) that a player controls are called a *force*.

◊ UNITS STAY TOGETHER

Units must be **Cohesive**, meaning that all models in a unit of 12 or less must be within 4" of each other *(see Figure 6)*. If a unit contains more than 12 models, all models must be within 5" of each other to be Cohesive.

If a unit ends an activation and is not Cohesive, it gains a point of Fatigue *(Fatigue is explained below)*.

A unit must also be kept clearly separate from friendly units if possible.

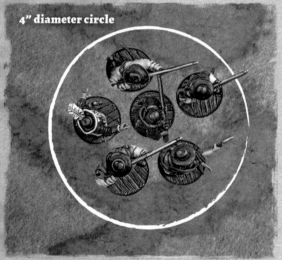

4" diameter circle

Figure 6: A Cohesive unit

◊ UNITS ACT TOGETHER

When a unit activates to take actions, all models in the unit take the same action. The next section of the rule book will give instructions on how to take actions with units.

Models in units have a 360° Arc of Fire. This means a model can act in any direction regardless of which way it is facing. Arc of Fire can become limited at times, such as when a unit is inside a structure or managing artillery. Those instances are noted in the applicable rules.

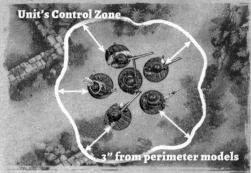

Unit's Control Zone

3" from perimeter models

Figure 7: A unit's Control Zone

◊ UNITS EXERT A CONTROL ZONE

Every unit has a **Control Zone** of 3". No enemy units may move into the Control Zone of an enemy unit unless they charge in to initiate a Melee Combat. This will be explained fully in the Melee Combat section.

◊ UNITS AND LINE OF SIGHT

Line of Sight is a fundamental mechanic in Blood & Plunder, and in miniature games in general. It is used to determine if models in units are able to "see" models in enemy units in order to attack them, usually with Ranged Attacks.

The easiest way to check Line of Sight during gameplay is to use a tape measure or ruler as a straight line, typically while measuring distances. This method will suffice for most situations; however, there will be times (such as when a target unit is partially hidden or at a different elevation) when it is necessary to determine what the model "sees" by looking low over the model's head. "Seeing" from a model's vantage point is called True Line of Sight.

A model has Line of Sight if it can draw an imaginary line straight from its base to its target's base, and that line does not pass through another unit or piece of terrain that would block it.

If a target model is partially obscured, Line of Sight can only be drawn if the torso of the target model is clearly visible. Assessing the True Line of Sight of a model is often the most useful way to determine if partially obscured models can be targeted.

Line of Sight traced from all the models in a unit is "added up" to assess how much of an enemy unit is eligible to be targeted *(See examples below)*.

Attacker

Defender

Figure 8

In Figure 8, at least one model in the attacking unit can draw Line of Sight to each model in the defending unit, except for the model around the corner of the chapel. Therefore, by "adding up" all the attacker's Lines of Sight, all the models in the defending unit can be targeted for a Ranged attack except for the one around the corner.

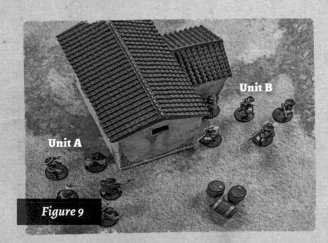

Unit B

Unit A

Figure 9

In Figure 9, Unit A and Unit B are on opposite sides of a small building. Unit A checks for Line of Sight from all its models to all the models in Unit B. It is determined that two models in Unit B are in Line of Sight, two models only have an arm and a leg visible apiece (therefore not in Line of Sight), and one model is completely hidden from view.

Models in a unit cannot trace Line of Sight through a friendly or enemy unit unless they are at a higher elevation *(See below)* or the unit they are tracing Line of Sight over is Prone (being Prone is explained under Actions in the next section of the rules).

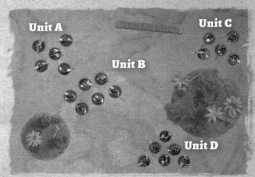

Unit A   **Unit C**

Unit B

Unit D

Figure 10

In Figure 10, all models in Unit A and Unit B can draw Line of Sight to all models in Unit C. No models in Unit A can draw Line of Sight to Unit D since the friendly models in Unit B are not Prone, thus blocking Line of Sight. Likewise, Unit D cannot draw Line of Sight to any models in Unit A.

If a unit is 1" or higher than another unit (either friendly or enemy), it may trace Line of Sight over that unit to target one behind it.

If a model in Line of Sight is obscured at all, it is usually considered to be in Cover. Cover and its importance will be explained in the Combat section.

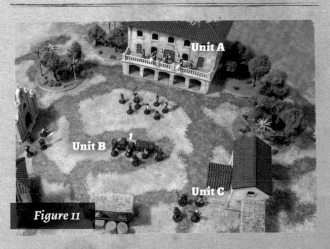

Unit A

Unit B

Unit C

Figure 11

In Figure 11, Unit A can draw Line of Sight to some models in Unit C because the balcony they are on is 1" or higher than Unit B.

UNIT CHARACTERISTICS

Each model type in the game has a unit card, which lists the stats of that model type. These are good to have on hand while fighting a battle.

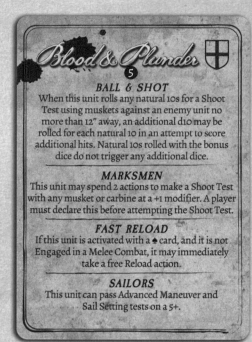

Each model in the game has:

1. an Experience level
2. a Point per Model value
3. a set of values reflecting its combat skills
4. Weapon options
5. any number of Special Rules

Though each type of model comes in a variety of poses, every model in a unit will use the stats as listed on its unit card.

Figure 12: *An example of a unit card*

◊ EXPERIENCE LEVEL

All models have one of three Experience Levels: Inexperienced, Trained, or Veteran. The unit will use its model's Experience level to determine how many actions it can take.

◊ POINTS PER MODEL

Each model type has a listed point value per model. This is only used when creating a force, not in the course of a battle.

◊ FIGHT (SKILL/SAVE)

A model's Fight value represents its ability to effectively land blows and defend itself in Melee Combat. This characteristic is split into two values; an offensive value (Skill) and a defensive value (Save).

The Fight Skill value is used to score Melee hits against an enemy. The Save value is used to defend against Melee hits inflicted by an enemy unit.

◊ SHOOT (SKILL/SAVE)

A model's Shoot value represents its accuracy with Ranged attacks and how well the model uses Cover as protection from Ranged Attacks. This characteristic is split into two values; an offensive value (Skill) and a defensive value (Save).

The Shoot Skill value is used to score Ranged hits against the enemy. The Save value is used to defend against Ranged hits inflicted by an enemy unit.

◊ RESOLVE

A model's Resolve value represents the ability to resist or remove Fatigue.

◊ WEAPONS

This is a list of all weapons the model is armed with. If a weapon is listed on the card as a Main Weapon, it can be used throughout the battle. A weapon listed as a Sidearm may only be used once in the course of a battle.

◊ SPECIAL RULES

Most units will have Special Rules to represent any specialties that unit might have. Special rules typically bend or break the normal rules of the game.

THE COMMANDER

A force's commander is its leading officer. Every force must include one (and only one) commander.

The commander's unit card is different because each force's commander must begin the game attached to one of the force's core units. The commander model is added to the chosen unit, and activates with that unit. The commander does not count against a unit's maximum size.

When a commander is attached to a unit:

> » the commander adopts the Experience Level, Fight Skill/Save, Shoot Skill/Save, and Resolve Value, and the Special Rules of the unit it is attached to.

> » the unit gains any Special Rules the commander has.

> » the commander has its own Weapons and Equipment.

> » if the commander leaves a unit, that unit loses any Special Rules the commander gave them, and the commander loses any that it gained from the unit.

The commander has Command Points and a Command Range, which are used to allow units to take extra actions. This is explained in Commanders and Command Points in the next section of the rulebook.

FATIGUE

Fatigue is a negative effect placed on units to indicate that their combat effectiveness has been reduced, usually from exhaustion or diminishing morale.

In Blood & Plunder, units may gain points of Fatigue when successfully hit in combat, or they may be intentionally given Fatigue when pushed to perform at a higher level in battle. The different ways that a unit can gain Fatigue and its consequences will be explained fully at the beginning of the Combat section, but for now know that:

> » A unit with 3 or more Fatigue points is Shaken, and is no longer effective in battle until it has less than 3.

> » A player cannot intentionally give a unit they control 3 or more Fatigue points (a player can never intentionally force one of their units to become Shaken).

> » If a unit ever has twice the amount of Fatigue points as it has models, the unit **Routs** and is immediately removed from the game. (*For example, a unit of 2 models with 4 Fatigue points would Rout*).

> » If any unit of any size has more than 6 Fatigue points, it Routs and is immediately removed from the game.

ENGLISH
BUCCANEER CAPTAIN
EXPERIENCED
15

May Command English Buccaneers

MAIN WEAPON: BRACE OF PISTOLS

COMMAND RANGE 8"

COMMAND POINTS 2

LEAD BY EXAMPLE

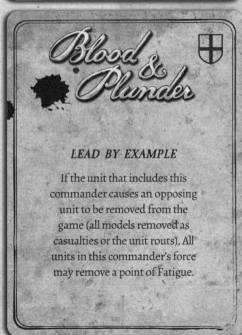

LEAD BY EXAMPLE

If the unit that includes this commander causes an opposing unit to be removed from the game (all models removed as casualties or the unit routs), All units in this commander's force may remove a point of Fatigue.

4
Activating Units & Taking Actions

n *Blood & Plunder*, players follow a card-driven process to determine the order in which units will activate, how many actions the units can perform, and what actions they will take. This section will explain that process.

4.1 Using Activation Cards to Determine Initiative.

1. DRAW ACTIVATION CARDS

Each player will use their own deck of playing cards (54 cards, including Jokers), referred to as Activation Cards. Before the game begins, each player should shuffle their own deck, and place it at the side of their play area.

At the beginning of the game (and at the beginning of every turn), each player draws cards equal to the number of their units currently on the battlefield. This hand of cards is kept secret, and no new cards are drawn until the beginning of the next turn.

Jokers will trigger random Events, the effects of which are found in the Scenarios section. If a Joker is drawn, consult the Events table (*p. 128*) and resolve it immediately. Draw another card to replace the Joker, unless an Event dictates otherwise. If multiple players draw Jokers, randomly determine (by a dice roll) which will happen first.

If a player does not have enough cards remaining in their deck to draw the required number of cards, shuffle all of the cards in the discard pile into a new deck and continue to draw from there.

2. CHOOSE A CARD AND PLACE IT FACE DOWN.

All players choose a card from their hand, and place it face down on the table. Once all players have placed a card, all cards are flipped over and revealed simultaneously.

If a player has fewer Activation Cards than another player, they have the option to pass. A player that intends to pass must still play a card facedown. That player then declares their intention to pass once all players have placed their cards face down, and returns the face down card to their hand without revealing it. The other players then reveal their cards as described above.

3. DETERMINE INITIATIVE BY CARD SUIT.

The strength of the suit will determine which player will activate a unit first. The hierarchy of the suits is:

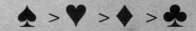

On the Activation Cards produced by Firelock Games, there are pips in the card suit to make it easier to tell which suit activates first. The suit with the most pips will win the initiative.

If players play the same suit, the card's value will break the tie (Aces are 1, Jacks 11, Queens 12, and Kings 13. All other cards use their printed values). If there is still a tie, both players roll a d10. The player with the higher result will go first. Re-roll further ties.

4. WINNER PICKS A UNIT AND TAKES ACTIONS

The player that played the highest-suited card picks a unit in their force that has not yet been activated this turn, and takes actions with it. A unit may be activated only once per turn.

The suit of the card that was played, and the Experience level of the chosen unit determines how many actions it can take:

	INEXPERIENCED	TRAINED	VETERAN
♠	1	1	2
♥	1	2	2
♦	2	2	3
♣	2	3	3

Table 1: Actions per Activation Card suit and unit Experience level.

There are circumstances that can increase or decrease the number of actions a unit can take, which are explained below. All the actions a unit can take are detailed later in this section.

A unit may take some, all, or none of its actions. Likewise, if a player played an Activation Card for a unit that was removed from the game before it had a chance to activate, that card may be discarded without effect if that player so chooses.

When the player has finished taking actions with the active unit, the player discards their face-up Activation Card, and the round is passed to the player that did not win initiative. Although it is not necessary, it is often helpful to place a marker next to a unit that has finished its activation so it is not accidentally activated again later that turn.

5. NEXT PLAYER PICKS A UNIT AND TAKES ACTIONS

The next player in initiative order (as determined by the face-up Activation Cards) activates and takes actions with one of their units as described in step 4.

If there are more than two players, continue to activate and take actions as described above in descending initiative order, until all players that played Activation Cards have activated one unit.

Once all players that played a card have activated a unit, the round is complete, and play proceeds to the next round.

6. REPEAT THE PROCESS, STARTING AT STEP 2 UNTIL ALL UNITS HAVE ACTIVATED.

If there are units in any player's force that haven't been activated, go back to step 2 to start another round. Follow the same process for determining initiative and taking actions.

Once all the units in each player's forces have activated, the turn is over. Start the procedure for the next turn over again at step 1.

If a player ends a turn and still has cards in their hand (usually because a unit was eliminated before it had a chance to activate), those cards are discarded before drawing a new hand at the start of the next turn.

4.2 *Gaining or Losing Actions*

FREE ACTIONS & THE ACTION LIMIT

Sometimes units will receive free actions during an activation. If an action is considered a free action, it does not count as an action for the unit, nor does it have any negative effect associated with it. The unit is considered to have taken that type of action, however.

For example, a unit with the Quick Special Rule uses a ♠ card to activate, so it can take a free Move action that activation. Therefore, the free Move does not apply to the Fatigue penalty associated with moving more than 8" in a turn. However, the free Move action still counts as taking a Move action.

In another example, a unit Charges an enemy unit to initiate a Melee Combat. A Charge action includes a free Fight action. If that unit takes another Fight action during that activation, it will gain +1 Fatigue point for taking a second Fight action during an activation, even though the one from the Charge was free (the penalty for taking a second Fight action is explained under Melee Combat, p. 47).

A unit may never take more than 3 Actions during an activation, unless the extra actions are free actions.

PUSHING UNITS

A unit that is activated may be Pushed to be given an additional Action, but that unit gains a Fatigue point as a result. A unit with 2 or more Fatigue points may never be Pushed and, as stated above, a unit cannot take more than 3 actions per activation.

THE NEGATIVE EFFECTS OF FATIGUE ON ACTIONS

» A unit with 1 Fatigue point is unaffected. It may take actions normally.

» If a unit begins its activation with 2 or more points of Fatigue, that unit takes one less action.

If this leads to a situation where the unit is reduced to 0 actions, the unit may only take a standard Rally action (which is explained under the Rally action description below).

» A unit with 3 or more points of Fatigue is considered to be Shaken, and can only take Rally actions (this is also explained under the Rally action description below).

Remember that Shaken units also have the -1 action penalty when activated because they have more than 2 Fatigue.

4.3 *Actions*

When a unit takes actions, each Action is declared and resolved one at a time. All available actions in Blood & Plunder are listed by type and then explained below.

COMPLETE LIST OF ACTIONS

◊ STANDARD ACTIONS

» Move

» Charge

» Go Prone/Stand

» Shoot (Ranged Attack)

» Reload

» Rally (if the unit isn't Shaken)

» Throw Grapples (ships only)

◊ DEDICATED ACTIONS

» Fight (Melee Combat)

» Dismount

» Spike Artillery

» Start Fire

» Rally (if the unit is Shaken)

» Repair

» Change Sail Settings (ships only)

» Advanced Maneuvers (ships only)

◊ ASSIGNMENTS

» Crew/Abandon Artillery

» Crew/Abandon Sweeps

STANDARD ACTIONS

Standard actions are quick, decisive battlefield maneuvers.

» Any number of Standard actions may be taken by a unit during an activation, and in any order a player desires. However, there are some instances (such as moving more than 8" an activation, for example) where there may be negative consequences for doing so.

◊ MOVE

For one Action, a unit may make a Move of up to 4". Moving through Rough terrain, in structures, and climbing imposes a -1" penalty to a Move action, which is explained fully in the Terrain section (*p. 60*).

Units are moved as a whole, but each model in a unit is moved individually, one at a time. To move a unit, measure from the front of a model's base in the direction you wish to move, and move that model so the front of its base is placed at the distance measured. Repeat this procedure with all models in the unit. A model may move and act in any direction regardless of which way it is facing.

Players are free to change the arrangement of their units as they move, but they must be Cohesive when finished moving to avoid gaining Fatigue points (*see Units below*).

Models can move through friendly units without hindrance, but all models in a unit must end any movement clearly separate from any other units to avoid confusion over where each model belongs.

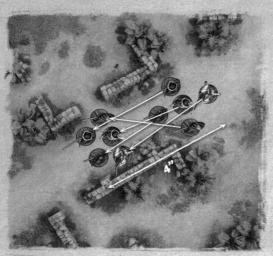

Figure 14

In Figure 14, a Unit takes a 4" Move action (shortened slightly) and changes the unit's shape. All models are within 4" of each other at the end of the move, so the unit is Cohesive.

A model may never move into or through an enemy unit's 3" Control Zone unless it is taking a Move to initiate a Melee Combat against it. This move is a separate action called a Charge, and it is explained fully in the Melee Combat rules.

A unit that moves more than 8" during an Activation gains a point of Fatigue.

◊ GO PRONE/STAND

For one Action, a unit may Go Prone in an attempt to better conceal itself. If a unit is Prone, simply lay one model on its side to signify it.

Mounted models cannot Go Prone; they must Dismount first to do so. A unit engaged in a Melee Combat cannot Go Prone under any circumstance.

A Prone unit receives a -2 bonus to its Ranged Save. A unit that is Prone may only take Rally or Stand Actions.

A unit remains Prone until it spends one Action to Stand. For the purposes of movement restricted actions, a unit that Goes Prone or Stands counts as having moved for the current activation *(for example, Artillery requires that its crew does not move in order to fire)*.

◊ CHARGE

A Charge is a type of Move action that initiates a Melee Combat with a unit, and is the only way that a unit may breach an enemy unit's Control Zone. A successful Charge move includes a free Fight action. Charges are explained in the upcoming Melee Combat section *(p.47)*. A Charge costs one action.

◊ SHOOT

A Shoot Action is used to attack an enemy unit from a distance. For one action, a unit may take a Shoot Test with one type of its ranged weapons (either Small Arms or Artillery). This will be explained fully in the Ranged Combat section *(p.53)*.

◊ RELOAD

For one Action, a unit may remove one Reload marker from one single type of ranged weapon (either Small Arms or Artillery) that unit possesses. No Test is required.

Units must take separate Reload actions to remove Reload markers from Artillery and Small Arms.

◊ RALLY (UNIT ISN'T SHAKEN)

For one action, a unit may try to Rally, which may allow a unit to remove Fatigue points. To Rally, roll a Test using 1 d10 for each point of Fatigue a unit has. The target number for the Test is the unit's Resolve value. A point of Fatigue is removed for each success.

For example, a unit with 2 Fatigue and a Resolve of 6 rolls 2 d10 for a Rally action. The results are 4 and 7. The 7 passes the test, so one point of Fatigue is removed from the unit.

A single Rally action is the only action a unit may take if it is reduced to zero actions due to Fatigue or other effects.

A unit cannot Rally during an activation in which it was Pushed to take an additional action.

◊ THROW GRAPPLES (SHIPS ONLY)

For one action, a unit on board a ship may throw grapples at another ship or other structure to pull them into contact. This is explained fully in the Ships section *(p. 88)*.

DEDICATED ACTIONS

Dedicated actions represent activities that require more time to perform.

» All Dedicated actions must be taken as the first action of a unit's activation, and prevent the unit from taking any further actions.

» If there is a Test associated with the action, each unused action (after the first) adds a -1 bonus to the associated Test.

For example, a unit activates with 3 actions. It chooses to Repair, which is a Dedicated action. The unit may take no other actions other than a single Repair action this activation.

Since it has 2 actions left after using one to Repair, the target number is a 5+ for the Repair Test, instead of the typical 7+.

» Dedicated actions do not trigger suit-activated Special Rules when the appropriate suit is played, unless dictated otherwise.

If the unit in the example above has the Fast Reload Special Rule (which gives it a free Reload action if it activates with a ♠), the unit does not get a free Reload action when it activates with a ♠ to take the Repair action.

◊ FIGHT

A Fight Action is used to battle enemy units in Melee Combat. As a Dedicated action, a unit may take a Fight Test against all units with which it is engaged. This will be explained fully in the Melee Combat section (*p. 47*).

◊ DISMOUNT

All models in the unit that are currently Mounted may dismount from their horses as a Dedicated action. When this occurs, replace the mounted miniatures on the table with models on foot (which may have different stats and special rules).

Once a unit has dismounted, it loses any Special Rules gained from being Mounted, and may not re-mount for the duration of the game.

◊ SPIKE ARTILLERY

As a Dedicated action, any unit that has models within 1" of an Artillery piece that is not being crewed by an enemy may attempt to destroy it.

Roll one d10 for the unit. The target number for the test is 7+. If successful, one Artillery piece within range cannot be fired for the rest of the game. The gun stays on the board as a terrain piece.

An Artillery crew can spike their own Artillery if they so desire.

◊ START FIRE

As a Dedicated action, any unit that has models within 1" of a structure may attempt to set it on fire.

Roll one d10 for the unit. The target number for the test is 10+. If successful, the targeted structure section is on fire.

See the Critical Damage tables in the Structures section (*p. 64*) for rules regarding fires. You may not use the Start Fire action to add more Fire markers to a section that is already burning.

◊ RALLY (UNIT IS SHAKEN)

A unit that begins an activation Shaken (with 3 or more Fatigue points) must Rally as a Dedicated action. It is resolved the same as described under Standard actions above, but follows the rules and receives the possible bonus from being a Dedicated action.

◊ REPAIR

As a Dedicated action, a unit may attempt to remove a Critical Damage effect from a structure the unit is currently next to or occupying. (The Critical Damage tables in the Structures and Ships sections will tell you what critical damage can be repaired).

The unit has to be in the same or adjacent section as the critical damage that it is attempting to Repair. If a unit is outside of the Structure it is attempting to repair, it must have a model within 1" of the damaged Structure section.

Roll one d10 for the unit. The target number for the test is 7+. If successful, the damage is repaired, and the Critical Damage effect is removed.

◊ CHANGE SAIL SETTING (SHIPS ONLY)

This Dedicated action is taken by a unit to increase or to decrease the speed of a ship. It is explained in the Ship Movement section (*p. 82*).

◊ ADVANCED MANEUVERS (SHIPS ONLY)

This Dedicated action is taken by a unit to attempt an Advanced Maneuver with a ship. It is explained in the Ship Movement section (*p. 86*).

ASSIGNMENTS

Assignment actions are similar to Dedicated actions, and are for assigning tasks to units that may last one or more turns.

» All Assignment actions must be taken as the first action of a unit's activation, and prevent the unit from taking any further actions that turn.

» Any unused actions that activation are wasted.

For example, a unit begins its activation with 2 actions. It chooses to crew an unattended gun battery. The unit spends one action to crew the guns, and the other action is wasted.

The unit is now considered to be crewing the guns for the rest of the game, or until another Assignment action is made for them to abandon the guns.

» Like Dedicated actions, Assignment actions do not trigger suit-activated special rules when the appropriate suit is played, unless dictated otherwise.

◊ CREW/ABANDON ARTILLERY

A unit may take an Assignment action to crew one or more Artillery pieces that do not currently have a crew. Likewise, a unit that is acting as crew for one or more Artillery pieces may take an Assignment action to abandon one or more of its guns.

Artillery and these assignments are explained in the Artillery section *(p. 72)*.

◊ CREW/ABANDON SWEEPS

A unit may take an Assignment action to crew the Sweeps on a ship that do not currently have a crew. Likewise, a unit that is acting as crew for the Sweeps may take an Assignment action to abandon them.

Sweeps and these assignments are explained in this section on Ship Movement *(p. 82)*.

4.4 Commanders & Command Points

A force's commander may spend Command Points to give friendly units additional actions. This is different than taking actions when activated with a card, because it can allow units that are not active to take actions!

While the commander's unit is active, the controlling player has the option of spending each of the commander's Command Points to give one action to one friendly unit within its Command Range. Spending a Command Point does NOT count as an action.

The Command Point action can be given to the active unit, or one that is not currently active.

If the unit taking the action is not currently active, then it acts immediately without any negative effects. *(see Figure 15)*

If the commander gives an extra action to the unit it is attached to (which is currently active), it counts toward the limit of 3 actions that a unit can take per activation. Since the commander's unit is active, there can be negative effects from taking the extra action.

For example, the commander's unit activates with 2 actions. It moves twice for a total of 8". The player uses a Command Point to give the commander's unit another Move action. This is legal, because the unit hasn't taken more than 3 actions while activated, but the unit takes +1 Fatigue point because it moved more than 8" during that activation.

Any action can be taken as an extra action — Standard, Dedicated, or Assignment. Using Command Points is a great way to get around the restrictions of Dedicated and Assignment actions, and any negative effects that are tracked during a unit's activation (remember, any action taken by a unit when it isn't active doesn't count against it).

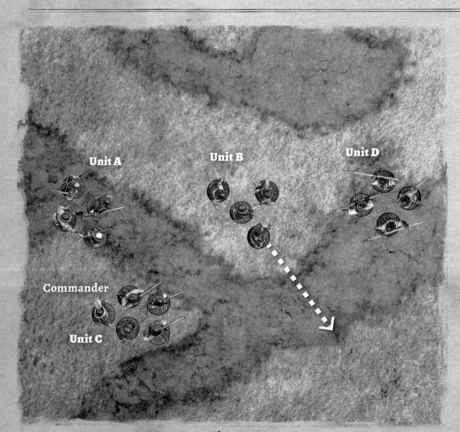

In Figure 15, Unit A would like to shoot at unit D. However, Unit B is blocking their Line of Sight to Unit D. Unit C is active and contains the commander. Since Unit B is within its Command Range, the player spends a Command Point to give Unit B a Move Action. This moves Unit B out of the way so Unit A can draw Line of Sight to Unit D. Unit B can activate normally later in the turn if it hasn't already done so.

Figure 15

For example, a commander may use one Command Point to have an assigned unit abandon a group of Artillery, then spend a second point to assign a different unit to crew the same Artillery.

In another example, the commander's unit activates with 2 actions, and attempts a Repair action. Although Repair is a Dedicated action, the unit may use a Command Point after the Repair is resolved to take an entirely different action (like Move, Reload, or Shoot, for example).

In yet another example, Artillery cannot be fired if it moved during an activation prior to firing. If a unit with an Artillery piece takes a Move action by a Command Point when it isn't active, then it does not count as having moved at the start of its next activation, and the unit may fire the Artillery as normal.

If the active unit is taking a Dedicated action, and a Command Point is spent to give that unit another Dedicated action, it is resolved as a completely separate action.

For example, the commander's unit activates with 2 actions, and attempts a Repair action at a -1 bonus. The unit fails the Repair Test. A Command Point to spent to give the unit another Repair action. This Test is rolled separately, and at the standard target number for the test (7+).

LIMITS ON COMMAND POINTS

A unit can only take one extra action from a Command Point per turn.

A commander that is attached to a unit that is Shaken can only use Command Points to take Rally actions with that unit until it is no longer Shaken. (Remember, a unit that begins an activation as Shaken can only take a Dedicated Rally action during that activation). Once that unit is no longer Shaken, the commander may use Command Points on that unit or any other friendly unit as normal.

A commander that is attached to a unit that is engaged in Melee Combat may only use Command Points to give extra actions to units involved in the same Melee Combat.

5
Combat

ombat falls into two categories: Melee (close quarters fighting) and Ranged (attacking from afar, with Small Arms or Artillery). The Fatigue Test, Melee Combat, Ranged Combat with Small Arms, and all the pertinent weaponry are described in detail in the following section.

Ranged Combat with Artillery is found in a later section of the rules, alongside Ships and Structures.

5.1 *Fatigue Tests*

A Fatigue Test is required when a unit receives any hits in Melee or Ranged Combat, whether models are removed as Casualties or not.

To take a Fatigue Test, a unit rolls one d10 if it has taken one or more hits, and an additional d10 for each casualty that was removed in combat. Units that have taken hits but have removed no casualties must still roll one d10 for a Fatigue Test.

For example, a unit took 3 hits, one of which was canceled with a Save, and removed 2 casualties. The unit rolls 3 d10 for its Fatigue Test: one for taking any hits, and two for the casualties.

The target number for the Fatigue Test is the Resolve skill of the unit that is taking the Test. For each failed Test roll, that unit gains 1 Fatigue point.

In the example above, the unit taking the Fatigue Test has a Resolve of 6. Three d10 are rolled, with results of 2, 3, 5. All three rolls failed the Test. The unit gains 3 Fatigue, which causes it to become Shaken

EFFECTS OF FATIGUE

» 1 Fatigue point has no effect on a unit

» 2 or more Fatigue points causes the unit to lose one action when it activates.

» 3 Fatigue points causes the unit to immediately become Shaken *(see below)*

» 7 Fatigue points or twice the number of Fatigue as models in the unit will cause the unit to immediately Rout (all models in the unit are removed from the game).

Units can attempt to remove Fatigue points by taking Rally actions.

5.2 Shaken Units

A unit that has 3 or more Fatigue points is Shaken. When a unit becomes Shaken, the player controlling it immediately chooses from one of two options:

> » **Fall Back**: the unit immediately takes a free Move action away from the enemy unit that caused it to become Shaken, moving around impassable terrain obstacles and enemy units.
>
> *or*
>
> » **Goes Prone**: the unit immediately goes Prone. *(See Standard Actions - Go Prone/Stand).* A unit engaged in Melee Combat cannot Go Prone (p. 41.)

Each time a Shaken unit gains more Fatigue points, it must again Fall Back away from the enemy, or decide to Go Prone. A unit that is already Prone must stay Prone.

If a unit Falls Back and reaches a table edge, the unit is Routed and all models in the unit are removed as casualties.

As mentioned earlier, a unit may never intentionally become Shaken by voluntarily gaining Fatigue points.

For example, if a player wanted to Push a unit with 2 Fatigue points to take an additional action, they could not do so because gaining an additional point of Fatigue for the Push would cause that unit to become Shaken.

Shaken units are not considered effective fighting forces. Units that begin an activation Shaken must take a Rally action as a Dedicated action *(see Actions p. 40)*, and that is the only action that unit may take that activation.

Actions that are triggered by other means (such as free actions that occur from a unit's Special Rules) may not be taken by a Shaken unit, unless that action is Rally.

BASIC TERMINOLOGY FOR THE COMBAT RULES

Cover and its effect on combat will be detailed in the Terrain section *(p. 60)* of the rules. For now, assume that a model usually has Cover if Line of Sight can be drawn to it, but there's something on the battlefield that a model can hide behind or hide in, which gives the model some protection from attacks.

A Defense Save (or simply a Save for short) is a Test taken by a unit to avoid taking Casualties. The target number for a Save in Melee Combat is the Fight Save value of the unit attempting the Save. The target number for a Save in Ranged Combat is the Shoot Save value of the unit attempting the Save.

A Save roll of natural 1 always fails and a roll of natural 10 always succeeds.

A **Casualty** is a model that has been permanently removed from the game as a result of attacks from enemy units or other effects.

Whenever a unit is the target of a successful attack (and after any applicable Saves have been resolved), it will remove a number of models equal to the number of unsaved hits scored against it. Models removed as Casualties may never return to the game for any reason.

Unless otherwise noted, Casualties are always chosen and removed by the player controlling the unit. This is important in situations such as when a player wants to keep his commander alive, or to keep models with unique weaponry on the battlefield. (For example, if there's one model in a unit that has Explosives, and it's removed from the battlefield, that unit no longer has Explosives!)

5.3 Melee Combat

In Melee Combat, units engage each other in bloody close-quarters fighting. All units can fight in Melee Combat even if they do not have a Melee weapon listed on their unit card.

◊ **TO INITIATE MELEE COMBAT:**

> » An attacking unit announces intent to move in to base-to-base contact (Charge) with an enemy unit.
>
> » The enemy unit may make a Defensive Attack, if applicable.
>
> » The attacking unit takes a Fatigue Test if it took any hits from the Defensive Attack.
>
> » The attacking unit moves into contact with and engages the enemy unit if it's not Shaken.

◊ **AFTER UNITS ARE ENGAGED:**

> » A Fight Action between the engaged units is resolved.
>
> » Fatigue Tests are taken by the defending unit if it took any hits
>
> » Players check to see if the Melee is over or if it will continue on a future Activation.

INITIATING MELEE COMBAT

1. Attacking player declares a Charge.

An attacking unit may move into base-to-base contact (Charge) with any enemy unit within its Move distance, even if the target unit is already engaged. A Charge cannot be made through a friendly unit in order to get base-to-base with an enemy unit.

The charging unit must declare which enemy unit is the target of its Charge before moving, as this will give the enemy unit an opportunity to make a Defensive Attack.

A unit may charge in any direction regardless of which way its models are facing.

Figure 16

In Figure 16, the unit on the left would like to initiate a Melee Combat with the unit on the right. It is within a Move distance, so it may do so.

2. Opposing player resolves any Defensive Attacks.

Units armed with Ranged weapons (most Small Arms excluding Explosives) have the option to deliver a **Defensive Attack** when they are charged. Units cannot make a Defensive Attack if they are already engaged in Melee Combat.

A unit making a Defensive Attack gains 1 Fatigue point, then attempts a Shoot Test against the charging unit before it begins its Charge move. Resolve a ranged Defensive Attack in the same manner as Ranged Attack (*see Ranged Combat with Small Arms p. 53*).

A charging unit may take Ranged Saves from a Defensive Attack if it began its Charge from Cover. Additionally, a charging unit cannot be the target of a Defensive Attack if the defending unit did not have Line of Sight to it when it began its Charge.

If the charging unit takes any hits from the Defensive Attack, the Casualties are removed immediately and may not be used in the Fight action as described in the next step.

The attacker must also roll a Fatigue Test if any hits are taken. If the charging unit gains enough Fatigue points to become Shaken, the charge move is cancelled, and Melee Combat does not proceed.

Figure 17

Continuing the previous example in Figure 17, the defending unit has muskets with no Reload markers, so it chooses to make a Defensive Attack with them.

The defending unit makes a Ranged Attack (which is fully explained later), and scores two hits on the attacking unit. The attacker fails both Ranged Saves, so two models are removed as Casualties.

The attacking unit must now take a Fatigue Test. Its Resolve is 5, and it must roll 3 d10 for the test (1 for taking hits + 2 casualties). The results of the roll are 3, 5, and 8, so the attacker gains 1 Fatigue point. Since the attacking unit is not Shaken, the charge may proceed.

3. Move the charging unit

A Charge is performed the same as a Move Action, with one exception as noted above: A Charge cannot be made through a friendly unit.

The charging unit must move as many models as possible into base-to-base contact with enemy models, closest models moving first. The attacker must have at least one model in base-to-base contact with the defender, or the Charge move cannot be made.

Match up charging models with unengaged defending models first, if possible; do not crowd on up a single defending model unless that is the only option. Those models that are unable to get into base-to-base contact should be moved as close as possible. The unit must be Cohesive at the end of the move. (*See Figure 18*).

Figure 18

If the attacking unit passes through another enemy unit's Control Zone to charge a different unit, it must also engage those units. (*See Engaging Multiple Units below*).

Once the Move is complete, the units are Engaged and the Activated unit takes a free Fight Action (*see below*).

4. Units resolve a Fight Action

A Fight Action is resolved as follows:

a. The attacking unit declares a weapon it will attack with, if any, and rolls one d10 for each of its models currently in the attacking unit (remember, some attackers may have been removed as a result of a Defensive Attack). The target number for the Fight Test is the Fight Skill value of the unit taking the test.

b. The attacking unit compares the results rolled for the Fight Test to their target number. Each roll that equals or exceeds the target number counts as a hit against the defending unit.

c. The defending unit may attempt one Melee Save per model in the unit, but cannot attempt more Saves than hits taken.

d. The defending unit rolls the appropriate number of Melee Saves as explained above. Roll one d10 per Save being attempted. The target number is the defending unit's Fight Save value. Any roll that equals or exceeds the target number cancels one hit.

e. Subtract the number of successful Saves from the number of hits taken. Any remaining hits are removed as Casualties, at the discretion of the defending player. However, there must always be at least one model

left in base-to-base contact with the attacking unit if possible.

Once the Fight Action is resolved, proceed to Step 5.

5. Defender rolls a Fatigue Test.

If the defending unit takes any hits in the Fight Action above, it takes a Fatigue Test. If the defending unit gains enough Fatigue at this point, it may become Shaken or Rout. Players should then check to see if all units involved are still engaged.

Units are no longer engaged when:

> » All friendly units or all enemy units involved in a Melee Combat have become Shaken and have moved out of base-to-base contact, and/or:

> » All enemy units in a Melee Combat have been Routed, and/or:

> » All enemy units in a Melee Combat have been removed as Casualties.

If the attacking unit (and possibly any friendly units) are no longer engaged at this point, it has the option to consolidate its models (moving them no more than 1") to form it back into a tighter unit, or maybe seek some Cover nearby. Friendly units that were previously involved in the Melee may consolidate even if they aren't activated. Consolidating does not count as a Move, and cannot be used to initiate a new Melee Combat. *(see Figure 20)*.

Attacker rolls 2 hits for the Fight Test

Defender fails both Saves, removes 2 Casualties

Figure 19

Continuing the previous example in Figure 19, The unit of 3 models (Fight 6/7) charged into an enemy unit of 6 models (Fight 5/6).

The attacking unit rolls 3 d10 for the Fight Test, with a target number of 6+. The results are 2, 7, 9. Two hits are scored against the defending unit.

With six models, the defending unit could potentially roll up to six Melee Saves, however, there were only two hits, and so it only rolls two Saves. Their target number to Save is 6+. The resulting rolls are 2 and 4, so the defending unit takes two casualties, leaving survivors in base-to-base contact with the enemy.

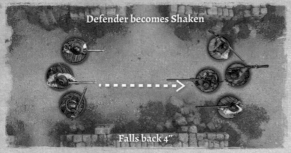

Figure 20

Continuing the previous example in Figure 20, the defending unit must take a Fatigue Test. The defending unit's resolve is 6, and 3 d10 are rolled for the test (1 for taking hits +2 casualties). The results are 1, 1, and 5, so none of the tests are passed. The defending unit gains 3 Fatigue points, and becomes Shaken.

Since it is now Shaken, the defending unit Falls Back (makes a free Move action away from the attacker) and is no longer engaged in Melee Combat. Since it is no longer engaged, the active unit may consolidate or follow the fleeing unit (see example below).

6. Check for Ongoing Melee Combat

If there are units that are still Engaged:

> » The active unit moves as many of its remaining models as it can into base-to-base contact with enemy models to fill in spaces that have been left by Casualties. All units must also be Cohesive at the end of combat.

> » These engaged units are now considered locked in Ongoing Melee Combat. When a unit engaged in an Ongoing Melee Combat activates in the future and takes a Fight action, follow Steps 4–6 above.

Remember, if a unit is fighting an Ongoing Melee Combat, the Fight action is a Dedicated action (*See Actions for the penalties and bonuses associated with Dedicated actions p. 41*).

Engaged units may only take Fight and Rally Actions until the units involved are no longer engaged.

When all involved units are no longer engaged, the Melee Combat has ended.

ENGAGING MULTIPLE UNITS

When a unit is engaged with multiple enemy units, Melee hits scored must be split between all opposing units as evenly as possible. All affected enemy units may attempt Melee Saves as normal.

PURSUING SHAKEN UNITS

When an engaged unit becomes Shaken and flees Melee Combat, any enemy unit previously engaged in the Melee with it may take a free Move action to follow it as long as it is not engaged with another unit.

Figure 21

In Figure 21, the victorious attacking unit may Move to continue Melee Combat with the newly Shaken unit it was just in Melee Combat with, so it moves 4" back into base-to-base contact.

If the Shaken unit and its pursuers still have models in base-to-base contact after they all move, they are still considered engaged and therefore locked in Ongoing Melee Combat.

This free Move to follow a Shaken unit cannot cross into the Control Zone of any enemy unit other than one that just fled Melee Combat. If it would, the pursuing unit can only consolidate instead.

SHAKEN UNITS IN MELEE COMBAT

Shaken units cannot attempt Melee Saves while Shaken.

PRONE UNITS IN MELEE COMBAT

If a Prone unit is Charged by an enemy unit, it may not attempt Melee Saves against the Fight action, but may Stand as a free Action.

TERRAIN AND MELEE COMBAT

Below are some situations where terrain may come in to play in a Melee Combat. Everything mentioned below that may seem unclear is explained further in the upcoming Terrain section (*p. 60*), or details about Cover can be found under Terrain and Ranged Combat.

Rough terrain are areas of the board that are harder to move through (suchh as rocky ground, shallow water, etc.) will slow a Charge Move (-1" to the Charge distance).

A unit can't Charge through Impassable Terrain. It must find an alternate route (either move around or climb over the terrain).

Figure 22

In Figure 22, two units are on opposite sides of a boarded-up house. To initiate a Melee Combat, either unit would have to either move around the end of the building, or climb over the top.

A unit can Charge an enemy unit while climbing, but the climbing unit is less effective. If a unit Charges another unit during a climbing Move action, the attacking unit has a +1 penalty to the free Fight action.

Cover from terrain provides a -1 bonus to Melee Saves, but only if it is Hard Cover (such as stone works and areas of sturdy construction), and only if all models in the unit are in Hard Cover.

Smaller obstacles (up to 1" high and 1" wide) can be ignored for blocking base-to-base contact in Melee Combat. Therefore, models that are engaged on opposite sides of a short barrier or small object are considered to be in base-to-base contact. Units separated in this way are always in Cover, so the bonus mentioned for Hard Cover above may apply.

RANGED ATTACKS INTO MELEE COMBAT

Ranged Attacks cannot be attempted if there is a chance that engaged units will take hits.

5.4 *Melee Weapons*
STANDARD MELEE WEAPONS

This weapon type represents one-handed Melee weapons such as swords, clubs, and boarding axes. There are no special rules for these weapons; they simply allow models to participate in Melee Combat effectively.

HEAVY MELEE WEAPONS

Heavy Melee weapons include more intimidating arms such as large war clubs, broadswords, and two-handed axes. They hit hard, but leave the wielder vulnerable.

A model armed with a heavy Melee weapon receives a +1 penalty to its Melee Saves. However, whenever that model hits with a Fight Test, it bestows a +1 penalty to the Melee Save of the model taking the hit.

PIKES, LANCES, AND BAYONETS

These long weapons give their wielder an opportunity to strike first, and are effective on offense or defense.

◊ **ON OFFENSE:**

All attackers with pikes/lances/bayonets bestow a +1 penalty to the defending unit's Melee Saves when charging.

◊ **ON DEFENSE:**

All these weapons may be used to make a Defensive Attack when a unit wielding them is charged, so long as the defending unit with pikes/lances/bayonets is not Mounted.

The unit making a Defensive Attack with a pike/lance/bayonet uses their Fight Skill instead of Shoot sSkill for the test, and the Defensive Attack is made after the attacker is in base-to-base contact, but before they roll their Fight Test from the Charge. Additionally, the defenders gain no Fatigue points when making a Defensive Attack in this manner.

◊ **DRAWBACKS:**

Wielders of these long weapons have the offensive and defensive benefits listed above against all other melee weapons, but the longer weapon takes precedence when they face each other.

Pikes are longer than Lances, which are in turn longer than Bayonets. As such, if two units armed with pikes, lances, or bayonets are charging each other, the longer weapon has the appropriate benefit, and the other does not.

For example, a unit with lances charges a unit with bayonets. Since the lances are longer, the charging unit will inflict a +1 penalty to the defending unit's Melee Saves, but the defending unit will not be allowed a Defensive Attack with the bayonets.

If two units with the same type of these weapons face each other, then all the abilities mentioned above are cancelled for both units.

For example, a unit armed with lances charges a unit that is also armed with lances. The attacking unit does not inflict a penalty on the defending unit's Melee Saves, and the defending unit does not have the option of making a Defensive Attack.

Due to their great length, a unit armed with pikes loses all the abilities described above it has models that are in confined spaces (e.g. area terrain that provides Cover or inside Structures). In that case, the models with pikes are considered to have standard Melee Weapons instead.

PISTOLS

Pistols are compact but inaccurate short-range black powder weapons, and are useful in close-quarters combat.

A unit armed with pistols that have no Reload markers may declare them as Melee weapons either during a Charge or when engaged in a Melee Combat. If used as Melee weapons, the pistols gain 2 Reload markers, and after rolling a Fight Test the attacker may re-roll all of the failed attack rolls for that unit. Using pistols in this way counts as taking a Shoot action.

◊ BRACE OF PISTOLS

Models armed with a brace of pistols are carrying several pistols, so reloading is not a concern. Models equipped with a brace of pistols do not gain Reload markers when they fire their pistols.

THROWN WEAPONS

This unit carries weapons (like axes or javelins) that can be thrown at the enemy during a Charge. They cannot be used to make an effective Ranged Attack, and cannot be used for a Defensive Attack.

A unit armed with thrown weapons may re-roll all of the failed attack rolls for the Fight Test made during a Charge.

5.5 Ranged Combat with Small Arms

Ranged weapons in Blood & Plunder fall into two categories: Small Arms and Artillery.

In game terms, Small Arms consist of all portable weapons carried by a single model, like muskets, grenadoes, pistols, and bows. Artillery are cumbersome guns that require multiple models to operate, but hit much harder.

In this section, we will just discuss making Ranged Attacks with Small Arms. Artillery will be explained in a separate section, later in the rules *(p. 72)*.

MAKING A RANGED ATTACK WITH SMALL ARMS

A Shoot action using Small Arms is resolved as follows:

1. Choose a target.

2. Check Line of Sight.

3. Choose a (loaded) weapon with which to Shoot.

4. Measure to determine range penalty.

5. Roll the Shoot Test.

6. Add Reload markers.

7. Enemy may attempt Saves if in Cover.

8. Remove enemy Casualties.

9. Enemy takes a Fatigue Test if hits/Casualties are scored.

1. CHOOSE A TARGET.

Choose an enemy unit to be the target of the Ranged Attack. (A ship's Rigging is also an eligible target, but that will be addressed in the ship section of the rulebook *p. 80*).

2. CHECK LINE OF SIGHT.

Check to see if each model in the shooting unit has Line of Sight to a least one model in the target unit. Only those models that have Line of Sight will be counted for the Shoot Test in Step 5.

If no model in the shooting unit has Line of Sight to the target unit, that unit may not be targeted. The shooting unit may select a different enemy unit as long as Line of Sight exists between them.

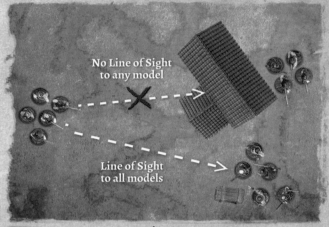

No Line of Sight to any model

Line of Sight to all models

Figure 23

In Figure 23, the unit on the left would like to make a Ranged Attack against the unit behind the building, but can't since the building completely blocks Line of Sight.

The attacking unit instead chooses to shoot at the unit partially behind the crate, because Line of Sight can be drawn from at least one attacker's models to at least one of the defender's. (or in this case, all of them!)

3. CHOOSE A WEAPON TO SHOOT WITH.

A unit making a Ranged Attack with Small Arms must declare which weapon it will use for the attack. Each model may only shoot with a single weapon per attack regardless of how many it carries, and may only attack with that one chosen weapon during an activation.

A unit can make a Ranged Attack with a variety of different Small Arms, but the controlling player must keep track of which weapons were used. Small Arms may be fired if they have 0 or 1 Reload marker *(See Roll the Shoot Test below)*.

A unit may make a Ranged Attack with Small Arms or Artillery, but never both in the same activation.

4. CHECK DISTANCE TO TARGET.

Measure the distance between the firing unit and the target unit.

Unless otherwise noted, all Shoot Tests receive a +1 penalty for every 4" the target is from the shooting unit.

Remember that unless otherwise noted in a Special Rule or in a weapon description, a Ranged Attack cannot be attempted if the target number for the Shoot Test is 11+.

Range	0" to <4"	4" to <8"	8" to <12"	12" to <16"	16" to <20"	20" to <24"	24" to <28"	28" to < 32"	32" to < 36"
Modifier	+0	+1	+2	+3	+4	+5	+6	+7	+8

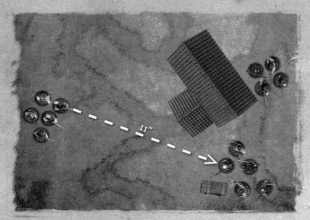

Figure 24

In Figure 24, the closest model in the attacking unit that has Line of Sight to the closest model in the defending unit is 11" apart. This will impose a +2 penalty on the Shoot Test.

5. ROLL THE SHOOT TEST.

If a unit with 0 Reload markers is making a Ranged Attack with Small Arms:

> » **All** models in the unit (if they all have Line of Sight) may roll one d10 for the Shoot Test, or

> » **Half** of the models in the unit, rounded down (if they all have Line of Sight), may roll one d10 for the Shoot Test.

If a unit with **1** Reload marker is making a Ranged Attack with Small Arms:

> » **Half** of the models in the unit, rounded down (if they all have Line of Sight), may roll one d10 for the Shoot Test.

The unit making the Ranged Attack spends one Action, and rolls the appropriate number of dice.

The first Shoot Test attempted by a unit during their activation is made without consequence. For every additional Shoot Test that unit attempts during their activation, the unit gains 1 Fatigue.

Compare the results to the Shoot Skill value of the unit, modified by the range. Each roll that is equal to or greater than the target number (Shoot Skill + range modifier) counts as a hit on the targeted unit.

Continuing the example shown above in Figure 24, Unit A has 5 models, a Shoot skill of 7/8, and is armed with muskets with 0 Reload markers. All models in the attacking unit have Line of Sight to all models in the defending unit, which is 11" away. The range penalty at that distance is +2, so the unit will hit on a 9+ (7 +2= 9). The unit chooses to fire with all its models, so it rolls 5 d10. The results are 2, 6, 9, 9, 10, which scores 3 hits.

UNITS SHOOTING WITH A MIX OF SMALL ARMS AND SHOOT SKILLS

When a unit makes a Ranged Attack with a mix of Small Arms, the different weapons are rolled for separately if they have different rules.

When a unit with a mix of Small Arms makes a Ranged Attack with half its eligible models, the player controlling the unit decides which weapons will be fired.

If the Commander is attached to a unit with a different Shoot value, and their target numbers are different, simply roll a different colored die or roll the test separately.

If the unit in the example above contains the commander, he would be armed with a pistol instead of a musket. In that case, the player controlling the unit could fire 5 muskets and the commander's pistol if they wished. The pistol would be rolled separately from the muskets if used, because the pistol has a greater penalty to hit.

6. ADD RELOAD MARKERS.

Small Arms that acquire Reload markers after a Shoot Test will receive them now.

> » If the unit made a Ranged Attack with all its models, it gains 2 Reload markers for that weapon.

> » If the unit made a Ranged Attack with half its models, it gains 1 Reload marker for that weapon.

The unit in the example above gains 2 Reload markers since it fired with all its weapons.

7. OPPOSING PLAYER ROLLS RANGED SAVES AND REMOVES CASUALTIES.

The defending unit may attempt one Ranged Save per model in the unit, but cannot attempt more Saves than hits taken.

The defending unit's Ranged Save value will differ when models are in and out of Cover. See Terrain and Ranged Combat below for exact details about determining Cover, but put simply:

> » Count the models in Cover first, and assign an equal number of hits to be saved using their Ranged Save values first. The target number of the Ranged Save of a model in Cover is the defending unit's Shoot Save value.

> » If any hits remain unassigned and there are models in the defending unit that are not in Cover, then apply a Ranged Save value of 9+ to each remaining hit for each model that is not in Cover.

Roll one d10 per Save being attempted, following the criteria above. If a unit is attempting Saves with different target numbers, either roll the Saves separately, or roll different colored dice for each to differentiate them. Each roll that equals or exceeds the target number cancels 1 hit.

Subtract the number of successful Saves from the number of hits taken. Any remaining hits are removed as Casualties, at the discretion of the defending player.

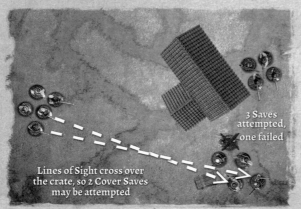

Figure 25

To continue our previous example in Figure 25, the attacking unit scored 3 hits. The defending unit has 2 models in a position where Line of Sight from the attacking unit passes over a crate, which is an object that provides Cover. Therefore, the defending unit may attempt two Ranged Saves with the benefit of Cover, and one Save without it.

First, Saves will be attempted for two of the hits using the Ranged Save values of the two models in Cover. The Shoot Skill of the defending unit is (5/7). The defending player rolls 2 d10. The results are 6 and 7, so one Save is made.

Next, the defending unit rolls the Ranged Save for the remaining hit using the Save value of a model in the open. The target number is 9+, and the defending player rolls 1 d10. The result is a 9, so another Save is made

Three hits – two Saves = one model of the defending player's choice will be removed as a casualty. Note that even though a Ranged Save in Cover was failed, the defending player chooses to remove a model that is not in Cover.

8. DEFENDING UNIT ROLLS A FATIGUE TEST.

If the targeted unit took hits (even if it suffered no Casualties) it must take a Fatigue Test, and may gain Fatigue as a result).

TERRAIN & RANGED COMBAT

Below are some situations where terrain may come in to play in a Ranged Attack. Everything mentioned below that may seem unclear is explained further in the upcoming Terrain section *(p. 60).*

◊ DETERMINING IF MODELS ARE IN COVER

Models are considered to be in **Cover** if a Line of Sight being drawn to them passes through or over a piece of terrain that a model can either hide behind or hide in. *(see Figure 26).*

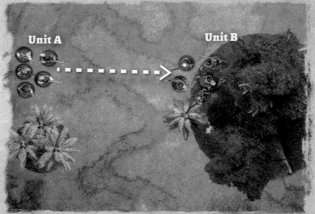

Figure 26

In Figure 26, Unit A is making a Ranged Attack against Unit B, which has three models hiding in a stand of trees. Unit B has three models that are in Cover from at least one model in Unit A, and two which are not in Cover from any model in Unit A.

◊ CASUALTIES AND LINE OF SIGHT

Unless otherwise noted, Casualties may be removed from any part of the unit that is in Line of Sight of at least one model in the attacking unit. Models that are not in Line of Sight are not considered when determining Cover, may not be assigned hits, and may not be removed as Casualties from a Ranged Attack *(see example below).*

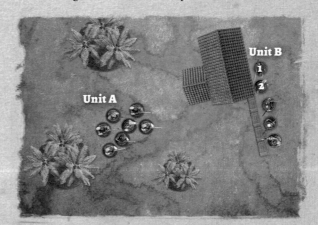

Figure 27

In Figure 27, Unit A is making a Ranged Attack against Unit B. Unit B has three models that are behind a low wooden wall and two models (labeled 1 and 2) that are behind a building and hence out of Line of Sight of Unit A. Only the three models in the defending unit that are in Line of Sight to the attacker may be hit, attempt Saves, or be removed as Casualties.

◊ COVER VS. HARD COVER

Most Cover is composed of softer materials such as light wood planks or dense vegetation, and provides the standard Ranged Save as determined by the Ranged Save value of a unit's Shoot Skill.

Tougher materials (like stone and the heavy timber of ship gunwales) are known as Hard Cover, and add -1 bonus to Ranged Saves to models that are using them as Cover.

To gain the benefits of Hard Cover, all models in a unit must be in Hard Cover. A unit that has models out in the open or behind a mix of Cover and Hard Cover will not receive the -1 bonus to their Ranged Saves.

◊ RANGED COMBAT FROM ELEVATION

As mentioned in the section on Line of Sight, a unit that is 1" or higher than another unit can trace Line of Sight through that unit to target a unit or Structure behind it.

Additionally, a defending unit on a lower elevation receives a +1 penalty to Ranged Saves from units making a Ranged Attack from an elevation of 2" or higher than the defending unit.

5.6 Ranged Weapons: Small Arms

Unless otherwise noted, all weapons listed below:

» Are used to make Ranged Attacks

» Can be used to make Defensive attacks.

» Gain 2 Reload tokens when fired.

MUSKETS

Muskets are the standard black powder firearm of European standing armies and come in several types (described below). All muskets are somewhat unwieldy, but accurate at a distance.

A Mounted model may not fire muskets (of any type); they must Dismount to do so.

◊ FIRELOCK MUSKETS

» Long Range: if the target number of a Shoot Test made with this weapon is 11+, but the target falls within 24", the Shoot Test will succeed on a natural 10.

◊ MATCHLOCK MUSKETS

» Long Range: if the target number of a Shoot Test made with this weapon is 11+, but the target falls within 24", the Shoot Test will succeed on a natural 10.

» Match Cords: glowing match cords give away the unit's position at night. Units can double the viewing to distance (24" instead of 12") to units armed with Matchlocks if the scenario takes place at night. A unit may extinguish their match cords with a Standard action to avoid this, but the weapons cannot be fired until they are relit. It requires the unit to take a Dedicated action to relight them.

◊ BUCCANEER GUNS

These are expertly crafted, long-barreled firelock muskets.

» Very Long Range: if the target number of a Shoot Test made with this weapon is 11+, but the target falls within 28", the Shoot Test will succeed on a natural 10.

◊ HEAVY MATCHLOCK MUSKETS

These large heavy guns are very accurate at longer ranges, but are quite cumbersome.

» Superior Range: if the target number of a Shoot Test made with this weapon is 11+, but the target falls within 32", the Shoot Test will succeed on a natural 10.

» Match Cords: glowing match cords give away the unit's position at night. Units can double the viewing to distance (24" instead of 12") to units armed with Matchlocks if the scenario takes place at night. A unit may extinguish their match cords with a Standard action to avoid this, but the weapons cannot be fired until they are relit. It requires the unit to take a Dedicated action to relight them.

» Heavy: a model may not make a Ranged Attack with this weapon if it moved or participated in a Melee Combat earlier in the current activation.

CARBINES

Carbines are similar to muskets but smaller. As a consequence, they have a shorter range. To represent this in the game, carbines do not have a chance to hit on an 11+ like muskets.

Carbines can be Matchlocks or Firelocks. The Matchlock version suffers the same nighttime penalties listed for Matchlock muskets *(see above)*.

PISTOLS

Pistols are compact but inaccurate short-range black powder weapons. All Shoot Tests receive an additional +2 penalty when making a Ranged Attack with a pistol unless the target is within 4", in which case the penalty is an additional +1 instead.

◊ BRACE OF PISTOLS

Models armed with a brace of pistols are carrying several pistols, so reloading is not a concern. Models equipped with a brace of pistols do not gain reload markers when they fire their pistols.

BLUNDERBUSS

A blunderbuss is a short range firearm that fires shot and other types of shrapnel.

All Shoot Tests receive an additional +2 penalty when making a Ranged Attack with a blunderbuss unless the target is within 4", in which case the penalty is an additional +1 instead.

A blunderbuss rolls 2 dice when fired, and when any natural 10s are rolled against an enemy unit no more than 12" away, an additional d10 may be rolled for each natural 10 in an attempt to score additional hits. Natural 10s rolled with the bonus dice do not trigger any additional dice.

BOWS

Bows are more primitive weapons than typical black powder weapons. They fire at a much higher rate but are much less powerful.

Ranged Attacks made with bows have an additional +1 penalty to the Shoot Test at any range. Additionally, models get a -1 bonus to Ranged Saves against hits caused by bows.

Unlike all other Small Arms, a unit using bows may make 2 Ranged Attacks per activation without incurring a Fatigue penalty. A third Ranged Attack in an activation would incur the usual +1 Fatigue penalty.

Bows receive no Reload markers when fired.

EXPLOSIVES

Explosives are considered Small Arms, with a few differences:

» They cannot be used for Defensive Attacks.

» They do not gain Reload markers.

» They cannot target Rigging.

» All explosives have a range of 5", do not need Line of Sight, and do not apply a range penalty. See Making an Attack with Explosives below for details on throwing Explosives.

» Each type of Explosive has a different effect. See the descriptions below to see how each type works.

A model equipped with Explosives must choose one of the three types listed below to use for the duration of the battle. A unit may have a mix of different types of Explosives.

Grenadoes: A unit throwing grenadoes rolls 3 dice per model equipped with them. The target number for the Shoot Test is 7+, and no additional bonuses can be applied to it.

When this unit rolls any natural 10s for a Shoot Test using grenadoes, an additional d10 may be rolled for each natural 10, to attempt to score additional hits. Natural 10s rolled with the bonus dice do not trigger any additional dice.

A unit hit by grenadoes cannot take any Saves against those hits.

Firepots: A firepot works like a grenadoe, except the target number for the Shoot Test is 8+, and Firepots do not score additional hits on natural 10s like grenadoes do.

Additionally, if thrown at a unit in a structure (or at a structure), roll a d10. If the result is 8+ apply a Fire critical damage effect on that structure section. *(See the Critical Damage Tables in the Structures rules section for the rules on burning structures p. 68).*

Stinkpots: A unit throwing a stinkpot does not roll any dice. Rather than targeting enemy units, stinkpots are used to target any point on the table or structure section within 5" of the activated unit. A stinkpot may not be thrown at the same location or in the same Structure section as an existing stinkpot smoke marker.

The target point becomes the center of a 3" diameter column of smoke. Place an appropriate marker at the location (poly-fil or some cotton works great!). The smoke provides Cover to any models that are in or behind it.

The smoke from a stinkpot is quite noxious. Any unit that enters a stinkpot cloud, or begins an activation in a cloud, must make a Resolve Test with one d10. A failed test causes the unit to gain a point of Fatigue. Units in a stinkpot cloud may not make any Ranged Attacks until the move out of the cloud.

The smoke column is removed from the table at the end of the next activation of the unit that originally threw it. If that unit is removed from the battlefield before that point, the cloud is also removed.

MAKING AN ATTACK WITH EXPLOSIVES

Explosives may be thrown up to 5" vertically, horizontally, or any combination of the two. Unlike typical weapons used to make Ranged Attacks, they do not need Line of Sight to their target, and do not incur a range penalty *(see Figure 28)*.

◊ MISFIRES

Explosive are dangerous and unpredictable, and unless care is taken, they can go off in the attacker's hand!

» If a unit with Explosives uses 2 actions to make an attack with them, there is no chance of misfire.

» If a unit with Explosives uses 1 action to make an attack with them, roll one d10 for each model attacking with Explosives.

On a roll of 1-2, the explosive detonates prematurely. Roll the appropriate dice for hits and/or apply any other effects of the explosive to the attacking unit instead of the target unit. Roll a Fatigue Test for any hits and Casualties as usual.

Figure 28

In Figure 28, two units are on opposite sides of a small Structure. The unit on the left may lob Explosives over the structure to attack the unit on the other side since the structure is 5" tall (or less) and the target unit is 5" (or less) away.

6
Terrain

errain is very important in miniature games. Aside from providing places to stay out of sight, Cover to increase the odds of survival, and objectives for Scenarios, it makes your game table look really cool!

The scenario being played usually dictates terrain placement. You can be as simple or as fancy as you like, so long as the terrain on the table accurately reflects the scenario. Blood & Plunder plays best with enough terrain to cover about 25 percent of the board for land and amphibious battles. Sea battles usually require less. See the Scenarios section for more information about setting up a game board with terrain.

Before the game begins, players should discuss the properties of all terrain elements on the table as is outlined below. This is to make sure they agree on the rules for each one. If players disagree, employ Sportsmanship to resolve any disputes.

6.1 Classifying Land Terrain

To classify the different terrain on the land side of the game board, both players pick the same terrain feature and decide the following:

1. IS IT A STRUCTURE?

If a terrain piece is a Building, Fortification, or Ship, it does not need to be classified. It has its own set of rules explained below in Structures and the upcoming Ships section *(p. 80)* respectively.

Externally, a Structure is a large object that blocks Line of Sight to units (and possibly other Structures) behind it. Players may decide that some Structures can be climbed *(see Climbing Terrain p. 63)*. Players may also decide that Structures can be "boarded up," so units cannot access their interiors.

Note that some terrain features (such as a ruined building with 4 standing walls, or a stockade pen) might be eligible to use the rules for Structures.

Figure 29: *A large Structure*

2. CAN MODELS HIDE BEHIND IT?

Examples of this type of terrain include barrels, crates, lone trees, stone walls, and fences. This type of terrain is referred to as **objects**.

If models can hide behind a terrain object, it will provide Cover at any distance. However, if a model in an enemy unit is within 3" of the object, Cover is forfeited unless a model in the target unit is within 3" of the object as well. (*See Figure 31.*)

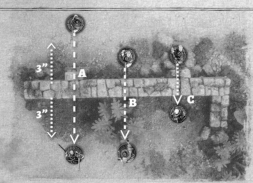

Figure 31

In Figure 31, the attacker on the top of the diagram is drawing Line of Sight over a low wall that provides Cover to a defender on the other side.
In A, the defender has Cover because both models are more than 3" from the object. In B, the defender does not have Cover, because the attacker is within 3" of the object. In C, the defender has cover because both models are within 3" of the object.

Shorter (up to about 1") terrain of this type will not interfere with Line of Sight, but it does impose a -1" penalty to each Move action used to cross it. Any terrain that slows movement by -1" per Move is called **Rough** terrain.

Taller terrain of this type could block Line of Sight completely, and would block movement unless players declare it is climbable.

3. CAN MODELS HIDE IN IT?

Examples of this type of terrain include planted fields, ruins, and stands of trees. This is type of terrain is called **Area** terrain.

If models can hide in an Area of terrain, it will provide Cover to all models on or within its boundaries.

Shorter (up to about 1") terrain of this type will not interfere with Line of Sight, but is usually considered Rough terrain.

Taller Area terrain (like a stand of trees) will incur the same -1" penalty to Move Actions, and will block Line of Sight to anything behind the Area of terrain.

Figure 32: *An example of Area terrain*

4. IF IT DOES NOT PROVIDE COVER, DOES IT HAVE SOME OTHER EFFECT ON GAMEPLAY?

"**Open**" areas of the board may have rules that affect gameplay, especially movement.

Sandy and rocky areas, as well as shallow water, are considered Rough terrain.

Deep water, fast water, or areas that are burning are considered impassable.

A large or complex terrain piece can have many of the traits listed above. (*See Figure 35.*)

Figure 30: Models seeking Cover behind some barrels

Figure 33: *Rough rocky terrain*

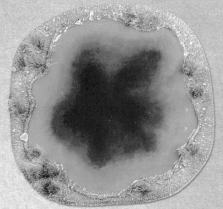

Figure 35

In Figure 35, the terrain piece has a pool of shallow water in the middle that can be considered Rough terrain, and several terrain objects that can provide Cover to models.

◊ **EXAMPLES OF TERRAIN TYPES DETERMINING LINE OF SIGHT AND COVER**

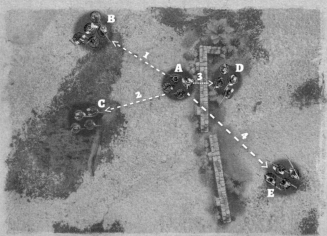

Figure 36

In Figure 36, units are checking Line of Sight between a forested area to the left and a section of low wall to the right.

1. A cannot draw Line of Sight to B, because B is behind an Area of terrain of large objects (tall trees) that block Line of Sight to anything behind it

2. A can draw Line of Sight to C, which is in Cover.

3. A and D both have Line of Sight to each other over the low wall, and both are considered to be in Cover since they are both within 3" of the wall.

4. A and E both have Line of Sight to each other. A is in Cover from E since it is within 3" of the wall. E does not have Cover from A since E is more than 3" away from the wall.

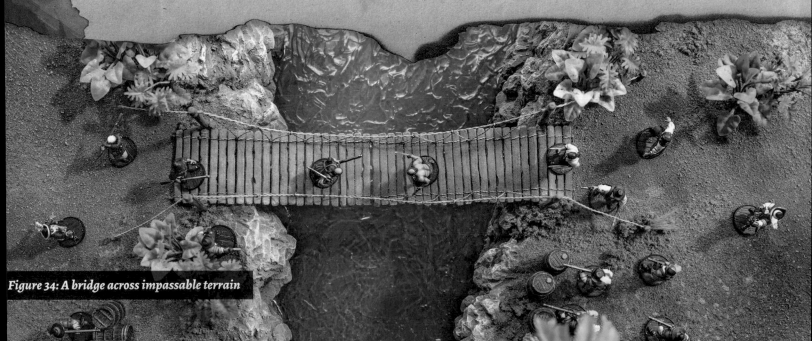

Figure 34: A bridge across impassable terrain

6.2 Classifying Navigable Water Terrain

To classify the different terrain that ships might navigate on the water side of the game board, both players pick the same areas and delineate the following:

DEEP WATER

Only Ships may move through deep water. Any model that enters deep water for any reason (such as a ship sinking) is removed as a casualty.

SHORELINES

A shoreline is the point at which the water meets the land. Most water within 3" of land is considered shoreline. A Ship that enters the shoreline will immediately Run Aground if it has a Draft value. *(See Ships p. 80.)* The shallow water along a shoreline is considered to be Rough terrain for models.

ISLANDS

An island is an area of land completely surrounded by water terrain. Islands can have other terrain elements on them. *(See Classifying Land Terrain above)* Islands are typically surrounded by an area of Shoreline.

SHOALS

A shoal is an area of exceptionally shallow water. Ships may move through shoals, but must Test to see if they Run Aground when they do so *(see Ships)*. Models that enter Shoals are removed as Casualties, just like models in Deep Water.

CLIMBING TERRAIN

If a unit wishes to climb a terrain feature, both players must first agree that the terrain piece is climbable. These rules apply to climbing up or down:

» To climb, a unit must begin the Move Action with all of its models within 1" of the terrain surface to be climbed.

» A -1" penalty to Move actions is applied when climbing.

» A unit can take as many consecutive climbing Move actions as it wishes (up to 3, of course). If it cannot reach a spot where it can place all its models by the end of the unit's Activation, the climb cannot be attempted.

» A unit can Charge an enemy unit while Climbing, but the climbing unit is less effective. If a unit Charges another unit during a climbing Move action, the attacking unit has a +1 penalty to the free Fight action.

Mounted models may not climb obstacles: they must Dismount to do so.

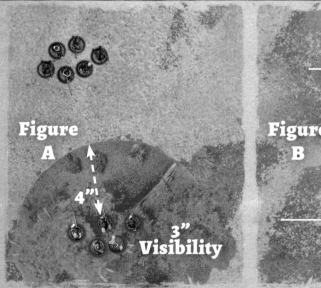
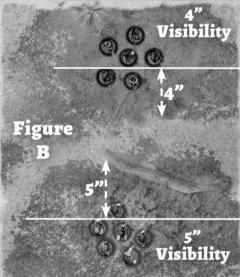

Figure 37

Consider Figure 37. In Figure 37A, the unit in the open cannot draw Line of Sight to the unit within the Area terrain since all models are more than 3" from the edge of the terrain from which Line of Sight is being traced.

In Figure 37B, both units have some models in Line of Sight to each other because those models are within the visibility range for the Area of terrain.

OPTIONAL RULE: LIMITED VISIBILITY

Limited Visibility is a scenario special rule that represents conditions where visibility is poor (e.g. fog, smoke, or darkness). This rule can also be applied to Areas of terrain (e.g. planted fields and forested areas) if the players wish.

Players decide how dense an Area of terrain is, and assign a range value to it in inches. The harder it is to see through, the lower the number.

For example, an Area of tangled jungle might have a visibility of 3", whereas a plot of palm trees in a village may have a visibility of 8".

The visibility range is how far a unit can "see" into or out of the given terrain. Units within the visibility range can be seen by other units, and are in Cover. Units beyond the visibility range are out of Line of Sight. *(See Figure 37)*

This rule can be applied to tall terrain instead of declaring that all tall Area terrain arbitrarily blocks line of sight to units behind it as stated above. *(See Figure 38)*

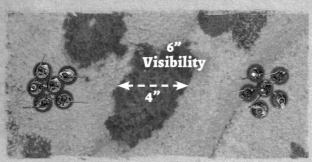

Figure 38

In Figure 38, the two units can draw Line of Sight to each other because the sparse Area of terrain is not wide enough to interrupt Line of Sight.

Congratulations! You have read far enough to know all the rules necessary to play a land-based game of Blood & Plunder. To make sure that you grasp the basics, we suggest that you stop reading the rules and play!

After you find an opponent, skip down to the Creating a Force section, and make a small force (no more than 100 points per player) with whatever models you have on hand. Then set up an all-land game board of around 3' x 3'. Put a lot of terrain on the table, evenly spaced, to provide plenty of Cover and shorten Line of Sight. If you do not have a lot of terrain, it might be a good idea to proxy objects or slap some together quickly out of craft materials.

Once that is complete, set up and play the Land version of the Encounter scenario. After a game or two, you should have a good grasp on the basics of Blood & Plunder. Then forge ahead to Structures and Artillery!

6.3 *Structures*

Structures fall into three categories

» **Buildings:** which encompasses everything from humble shacks to large stone structures like churches.

» **Fortifications:** including forts, gun emplacements, walls, and other defensible construction.

» **Ships:** all ships and boats, large and small.

The rules listed below apply to all Structures. Ships have additional rules that will be explained in a later section (p. 80), but everything here applies to Ships as well.

6.4 *Structure Basics*
STRUCTURE SECTIONS

Structures are made up of one or more sections.

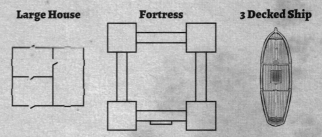

Figure 39: *Examples of how ships, fortifications, and buildings are divided into sections*

» **In Buildings:** each floor and/or room in the building is a different section.

» **In Fortifications:** each wall section, emplacement, and/or bastion is a different section.

» **In Ships:** each deck is considered a different section.

Structure sections do not have to be spaces clearly defined by walls. Large spaces (like the inside of a barn or the top of a fort wall) should be divided into sections before the start of the game. Divide the space into sections close to 4" x 4", but it does not need to be exact *(see Figure 40)*.

Regardless of their actual size, all Structure sections are considered to be 4" x 4" for the sake of range, movement, Command Actions, etc.

Structures usually have walls and roofs, of course, but sections can also be open-topped. Open topped sections are usually areas with low walls and no roofs, like the top of a fort wall, or the deck of a ship.

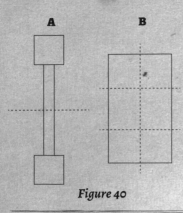

Figure 40

In figure 40A, a 9" long section of narrow wall connects two towers. The players decide that the wall should be divided into two 4.5" sections

In figure 40B, players decide to split an 11" x 7" barn into six 3.66" x 3.33" sections, because each section is reasonably close to 4" x 4".

UNITS IN A STRUCTURE

No more than two friendly units can occupy each section of a Structure. All models occupying a section must be able to fit in the section without their bases overlapping.

Because units in a Structure section are considered to occupy the whole section, the position of models is unimportant. As such, units inside a structure section ignore the rules for being Cohesive. Also, units that share a structure section need not remain clearly separate (*see Unit Basics p. 33*). It is good practice, however, to keep units as separate as possible.

A unit's Control Zone does not extend past the boundaries of the section they are occupying. This means that a unit can be within 3" an enemy unit if they are in adjacent Structure sections.

A unit cannot occupy more than one section of a Structure at a time, unless the unit is involved in a Melee Combat between sections (this is explained below under Structures and Melee Combat *p. 66*).

MOVING IN AND OUT OF STRUCTURES

To enter a Structure:

» A unit must have all models within 3" of the Structure to be entered, with at least one model in base contact with an access point (such as a door or window). The unit then takes a Move action with a -1" penalty to move into the section to which the access point is connected.

» For open-topped structures, models may enter from anywhere along the Structure's edge. This may require a climbing action if the height of the structure is too great. (*see Climbing Terrain p. 63.*)

» A unit may not end a move in a section unless all of its models can be placed inside the section without their bases overlapping.

» A unit may not end a move in a section if it contains 2 friendly units (but it may move through the section to another one).

» A unit may not enter a Structure section if it contains any enemy units, unless it is to initiate a Melee Combat .

To exit a Structure:

» A unit inside a section takes a Move Action with a -1" penalty to move through a wall with an access point to the outside the Structure.

» For open-topped structures such as Ships and some Fortifications, models may exit from anywhere along the Structures edge. This may require a climb Action if the height of the structure is too great (*see Climbing Terrain p. 63*).

» At the end of the Move action, the entire unit must be within 3" of the section from which it exited.

MOVING WITHIN A STRUCTURE

» Structure sections are always considered to be 4" wide, therefore a unit may only move one section for each Move Action taken.

» In order to Move through adjacent sections, they must have an access point (like a door) between them, or must be open-topped.

» A unit may not end a move in a section unless all of its models can be placed inside the section without their bases overlapping.

» A unit may not end a move in a section if it contains two friendly units (but it may move through the section to another one).

» A unit may not enter a Structure section if it contains any enemy units, unless it is to initiate a Melee Combat .

SHAKEN UNITS WITHIN STRUCTURES

When a unit in a structure become Shaken, it may either Go Prone or Fall Back as usual. If it Falls Back, it can either exit the structure via an access point, or retreat to an available adjacent section.

If a unit must Fall Back and is unable to do so (e.g. a unit fleeing Melee Combat into a fully occupied adjacent section), the unit Routs and all models in the unit are removed as Casualties.

6.5 Structures & Combat

STRUCTURES & MELEE COMBAT

To initiate Melee Combat with a unit inside a Structure:

» The charging unit must have all its models within 3" of the Structure section that contains the target unit, and the section must be open-topped or have access points (*see Figure 41*).

» The charging unit then takes a Move Action and moves as many models as possible into base contact with the section's exterior near any access points. The unit(s) inside the section may attempt a Defensive Attack, following the standard rules.

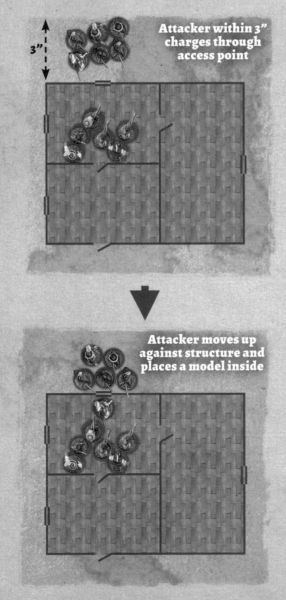

Figure 41: Initiating a Melee Combat with a unit in a Structure

» Instead of moving any miniatures into true base-to-base contact with the defending unit, place one model from the charging unit in the section to represent that the two units are now engaged. (This model is still considered to be part of the charging unit and fights normally).

» If there are two enemy units in the Structure section being charged, the charging unit will become engaged in Melee Combat with both units.

Only two outside units can be Engaged with the units fighting in the section at one time. If two units from outside the section are already involved, another unit cannot charge into that section (*see Figure 42*).

Once the units have become engaged, follow the standard Melee Combat rules for resolving it (*see Melee Combat p. 47*).

Once a section is clear of enemy units (because they have fled from being Shaken, have been Routed, or have all been removed as Casualties), the units that won the combat may use their consolidation Move to occupy the newly cleared section.

A unit may charge out of a Structure as if it were exiting normally (*See Moving in and out of Structures above*).

A unit that initiated a Melee Combat from either outside

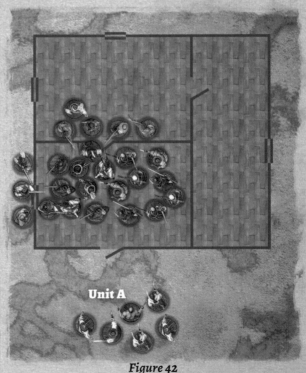

Unit A

Figure 42

In Figure 42, Unit A would like to charge in to join the Melee Combat, but cannot since two other units are already Engaged with the units in that section.

a Structure or from an adjacent section counts as having models in the section where the Melee Combat is taking place, and in the location that the charge originated from (*see Figure 43*).

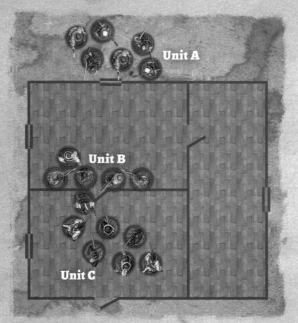

Figure 43

In Figure 43, Unit B is in an ongoing Melee Combat with Unit C. Unit A wishes to charge unit B, and may do so since Unit B is considered to have models in the section with Unit C and in the section that Unit B initiated the combat from.

6.6 Structures and Ranged Combat

LINE OF SIGHT FROM A STRUCTURE SECTION

Units in a Structure section are considered to have Line of Sight out from all access points in that section. Models have an 180° view from an access point.

Units in an open-topped section have a 360° field of view (provided they can see over the walls, of course).

Some Structures will have places from which models can draw Line of Sight that are not access points (like loopholes in the wall of a fort)

Figure 44: *A model's Arc of Fire from an access point*

MAKING RANGED ATTACKS AT UNITS IN STRUCTURES

A unit in a Structure may only be targeted for a Ranged Attack if Line of Sight can be drawn between the two units without obstruction from another section. Units in adjacent sections are always considered to have Line of Sight to each other as long as there is an access point between them.

Structure sections count as being 4" wide for the purposes of determining range, and as with all measurements, ranges between sections are measured from the two closest points between them *(see Figure 45)*.

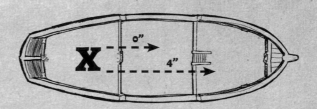

Figure 45

In Figure 45, the unit in the quarterdeck (marked X) is adjacent to the middle deck, so the range is 0". The foredeck is separated by the middle deck, and since all sections are considered to be 4", any unit on the foredeck would be 4" away.

Only Small Arms (and Swivels) can target units inside a Structure. Cannons can target Structure sections, which explained in the next section of rules (p. 76).

When a unit makes a Ranged Attack against a Structure section that contains multiple units, the hits must be distributed as evenly as possible between all units in that section.

If a section contains a unit that is Prone and one that is not, more hits must be applied to the unit that is not Prone, if possible.

For example, a deck on a ship contains two units. One is Prone, and one is not. The units on the deck are the target of a Ranged Attack, and 5 hits are scored. three hits must be applied to the unit that is not Prone, and 2 hits are applied to the unit that is.

All models in a Structure section are considered to be in Cover.

6.7 *Critical Damage Tables*

A structure can only be destroyed by taking Critical Damage. Taking hits from Artillery is the main way that Structures receive Critical Damage, but other things (like Firepots and the Start Fire action) can accomplish this as well.

When Critical Damage to a Structure must be determined, roll on the appropriate table below. We've included the Ship Critical Damage tables here as well, so you can find them all in one place when you need them.

Please note that some Critical Damage can be removed with a Repair action. If it can, it will be noted in the damage description.

BUILDING CRITICAL DAMAGE

10: TOTAL COLLAPSE

The entire building falls apart and becomes an Area of impassable terrain that blocks Line of Sight. All models within the building are removed as Casualties.

8–9: FIRE

The section targeted by the attack catches fire. Place a Fire marker on the section

Any unit that enters or begins an activation in a burning section must make a Resolve Test with one d10. A failed test causes the unit to gain a point of Fatigue. Units in a burning section may not make any Ranged Attacks.

A successful Repair action made by a unit in a burning section extinguishes the fire in that section and removes the marker.

At the end of the turn, roll a d10. On a 7+, the fire spreads. A section that is not burning but is adjacent to a section with a Fire marker on it is chosen at random, and a Fire marker is placed on it. A fire will not spread from a section if that Fire marker was placed there late in the turn, and the structure owner didn't have any units left to activate to try to put out the fire.

A structure may not have more than one Fire marker on each section. If a section were to gain a second fire marker, the structure is destroyed (*see Total Collapse above*).

2–7: DEBRIS

One model in the struck section is immediately removed without a Save (defending player's choice). If there are no models in the struck section, treat this as No Effect.

1 OR LESS: NO EFFECT

FORTIFICATION CRITICAL DAMAGE

10: BREACH

Place a 4" breach marker anywhere along the section targeted by the Artillery. This 3" area of scattered rubble is considered to provide Hard Cover and slows movement by -1" per Move Action. The breach also leads to the Fortification's interior (the area or section directly behind the breach). If any models are within that section, d5 of them take hits (Ranged Saves are allowed).

9: FIRE

The section targeted by the attack catches fire. Place a Fire marker on the section

Any unit that enters or begins an activation in a burning section must make a Resolve Test with one d10. A failed test causes the unit to gain a point of Fatigue. Units in a burning section may not make any Ranged Attacks.

A successful Repair action made by a unit in a burning section extinguishes the fire in that section and removes the marker.

At the end of the turn, roll a d10. On a 7+, the fire spreads. A section that is not burning but is adjacent to a section with a Fire marker on it is chosen at random, and a Fire marker is placed on it. A fire will not spread from a section if that Fire marker was placed there late in the turn, and the structure owner didn't have any units left to activate to try to put out the fire.

A structure may not have more than one Fire marker one each section. If a section were to gain a second fire marker, the structure is destroyed (all models are removed as Casualties, and the structure becomes an area of impassable terrain that blocks Line of Sight).

6–8: GUN DESTROYED

An Artillery piece is chosen and removed from the struck section by the player controlling the Fortification. It must be a gun within the attacker's Arc of Fire, and must be one facing the attacker, if possible. If not, remove a different gun.

If no gun can be removed, remove a model in the line of fire as a casualty (without a Save) instead. If there are no models to remove, treat it as No Effect.

2–5: DEBRIS

One model in the struck section is immediately removed without a Save (defending player's choice). If there are no models in the struck section, treat this as No Effect.

1 OR LESS: NO EFFECT

SHIP HULL CRITICAL DAMAGE

Ships with 1 section (Boats) have a simplified Critical Damage table due to their small size and simple construction. That table is found below.

10: CATASTROPHIC DAMAGE

The ship shudders and threatens to fall apart. The force associated with the ship gains a Strike Point at the end of this turn. (Strike Points and Strike Tests are explained in the Scenarios section *p.133.*)

The ship gains a Leak marker *(see below)*, and then the player rolls again on this table, and applies a second critical damage result. If the second result is a 10, the powder magazine of the ship explodes. Remove the ship from the board, and remove all units on it as Casualties.

Any other Structure section that is touching the ship when it explodes (like a dock or the deck of a grappled ship) will catch fire on a d10 roll of 8+. See the Fire Critical Damage result below.

9: FIRE

The deck targeted by the attack catches fire. Place a Fire marker on the deck, or an adjacent deck if the targeted deck already has one.

Any unit that enters or begins an Activation on a burning deck must make a Resolve Test with one d10. A failed test causes the unit to gain a point of Fatigue. Units on a burning deck may not make any Ranged Attacks.

A successful Repair action made by a unit on a burning deck extinguishes the fire in that section and removes the marker.

At the end of the turn, roll a d10. On a 7+, the fire spreads. The ship owner chooses a deck that is not already on fire, and places a Fire marker on the newly-burning deck. A fire will not spread from a section if that Fire marker was placed there late in the turn, and the ship owner didn't have any units left to activate to try to put out the fire.

A ship may not have more than one Fire marker on each deck. If a deck were to gain a second fire marker because all decks are burning, the ship is Destroyed.

A fire can spread to a ship that is fouled with *(see Collisions p. 87)* or connected via grapples to a burning ship, but only when the original ship has fire markers on all of its decks.

8: STEERAGE

The ship's steering is damaged. Add a Damage marker to the ships Steerage.

If the Steerage has one Damage marker, the ship's turn value is reduced by half (rounded down).

If the Steerage has two Damage markers, the ship no longer moves under sail normally. It will instead drift 3" or at its current Sail Setting when it moves, whichever is less.

If the ship already has two Damage markers on the Steerage, no more markers can be added, and the Hull of the ship takes an additional point of Damage instead.

One steerage Damage marker can be removed by each successful Repair action.

6–7 GUN

An Artillery piece is chosen and removed from the struck deck section by the player controlling the Ship. It must be a gun within the attacker's Arc of Fire, and must be one facing the attacker, if possible. If this is not possible, remove a different gun.

If no gun can be removed, the ship's hull receives an additional point of damage) instead.

4–5: LEAK

The deck targeted by the attack suffers a major leak. Place a Leak marker on that deck targeted, or an adjacent deck if the targeted deck already has one.

Leak markers do not have any effect on units.

A successful Repair action made by a unit on a leaking deck repairs the Leak in that section and removes the marker.

At the end of the turn, roll a d10 only if no attempt was made to repair the Leak that turn. On a 7+, the ship takes on water. The ship owner chooses a deck that is not already leaking, and places a Leak marker on the new deck. A ship will not take on water if that Leak marker was placed there late in the turn, and the ship owner didn't have any units left to activate to try to fix the leak.

A ship may never have more than one Leak marker per section. If a ship were to ever be forced to take more than 1 Leak marker on a section because all sections have Leak markers, the ship starts to sink. *(See Sinking Ships below.)*

◊ SINKING SHIPS

When a ship (not a boat) starts to sink, it is destroyed at the end of the next full turn. During the time while the ship is sinking, units on the ship may take actions as normal to try to escape, but may not attempt any Ranged Attacks.

A sinking ship cannot be sailed or rowed, and can only drift (unless it was Anchored).

A ship that has Run Aground does not sink, but the same rules apply. (The ship slowly breaks apart while being battered by wind and sea.)

When a ship sinks at the end of the turn, the ship is removed from the board and all units still onboard are removed as Casualties.

Any units on the sinking ship that are engaged in a Melee Combat with another ship are not removed as Casualties when the ship sinks, but if they become Shaken in the course of that Melee Combat , they automatically Rout. (In essence, they are clinging to the rail of the enemy ship as theirs goes under!)

2–3: RIGGING CRITICAL HIT.

Roll once on the Ship Rigging Critical Damage table. Apply any effects to the mast on the targeted deck. If the deck section does not contain a mast, the Hull takes an additional point of damage instead.

1 OR LESS: NO EFFECT

SHIP RIGGING CRITICAL DAMAGE

10: MAST DESTROYED

One of the ship's masts is shattered and falls into the water, impeding ship movement until the lines are cut away.

Place a Mast Destroyed marker on the deck containing the targeted mast. As long as that marker is there, the ship is immobilized and can only drift (unless Anchored or Run Aground).

The Mast Destroyed marker can be removed by a successful Repair action taken by a unit on the affected deck.

When the marker is removed, the ship immediately loses its highest Sail Setting. This effect is cumulative If multiple masts are lost. If a ship has no masts left, it is immobilized.

7–9: SHEETS & SHROUDS

Some of the ship's control or support lines have been severed. Place a Sheets & Shrouds Damage marker on the ship. Apply a -1 modifier to all Advanced Maneuvers or Sail Settings tests for each of these markers the ship has.

One marker may be removed with each successful Repair action.

1–6: SAIL & SPAR DAMAGE

The ship's sails or spars have taken significant damage. Place a Sail & Spar Damage marker on the ship. The affected ship's current Sail Setting is reduced by 1" for each of these markers the ship has taken. A ship cannot take more Sail & Spar Damage markers than the value of its maximum Sail Setting. (So a ship with a maximum Sail Setting of 5" can't take more than five Sail & Spar Damage marker.)

One marker may be removed with each successful Repair action.

0 OR LESS: NO EFFECT

BOAT CRITICAL DAMAGE

10: DESTROYED

The boat suffers catastrophic damage. It falls apart and sinks to the bottom of the sea. The ship is removed from the board and all units on board are removed as Casualties.

6–9: RIGGING DESTROYED

The boat's rigging is ripped away. The boat may not move under sail for the rest of the battle.

If the boat does not have Rigging, or it has already been lost, this result does an additional point of damage to the Hull instead.

2–5: LEAK

The boat suffers a major leak. Place a Leak marker on the boat.

Leak markers do not have any negative effect on units.

A successful Repair action made by a unit on a leaking boat repairs the Leak and removes the marker.

At the end of the turn, roll a d10 only if no attempt was made to repair the leak that turn. On a 7+, the ship takes on water and sinks. A ship will not take on water if that Leak marker was placed there late in the turn, and the ship owner didn't have any units left to activate to try to fix the leak.

If the boat has a Leak marker, and it is forced to take another Leak marker for any reason, it immediately sinks.

If the boat sinks, remove the boat from the board, and all units in the boat are removed as Casualties.

1 OR LESS: NO EFFECT

7
Artillery

rtillery have a variety of rules to represent the strengths and weakness of these big, powerful guns. Artillery come in 2 types:

» **Cannon** (which come in Light, Medium, or Heavy varieties) and
» **Swivel Guns** (or Swivels for short).

Artillery can either be attached to a Structure, like a Fortification or a Ship, or taken by a unit on mobile field carriages.

7.1 *Artillery Crews*

All Artillery must have a dedicated crew. As a crew takes Casualties, operating the guns becomes less efficient, and another crew may be assigned to take their place if necessary.

Each single piece of Artillery has a crew requirement, and the larger guns require more crew. *(See the Artillery Stats chart below.)* Only one crew model is required to fire a piece of Artillery of any type, but the minimum number of models required to effectively Reload and move them (if they can be moved at all) varies.

A unit is assigned to crew a group of Artillery before the start of a battle. This unit is the only one that may move, Reload, or fire those Artillery pieces until another unit is assigned to take their place. Units assigned to crew Artillery do NOT need to have the Artillery Crew or Expert Artillery Crew Special Rules (these units are just better at it!).

A unit may be assigned any number or ype of Artillery pieces, even it's more than it can effectively crew. When a group of guns is fired, moved, or Reloaded by the gun crew, the controlling player decides which ones are used.

For example, a unit of 4 models is assigned to 4 Light Cannons on a ship's deck (2 facing starboard, 2 facing larboard). Since the minimum crew requirement for Light Cannon is 2 models per gun, all four guns cannot be effectively crewed at the same time by the assigned unit.

The controlling player activates the gun crew, and decides to fire the two guns on the starboard side. This is legal, since there is at least one crew model for each of the guns being fired. The player resolves the Shoot Test as normal, and the guns gain 4 Reload markers.

On the next turn, the player activates the same gun crew, and would like to Reload the Cannons that fired in the previous turn. Since the minimum crew requirement is met for both of the guns that require Reloading (2 crew models per Light Cannon), they both may be Reloaded without penalty.

If the Artillery is in a Structure, all the guns assigned to a unit must be in the same Structure section.

Artillery crews must remain Cohesive with their Artillery pieces to move, reload, and fire them. Mounted units cannot crew Artillery.

7.2 Switching Crews & Abandoned Artillery

Artillery assignments may be changed by taking an Assignment action (see Actions). Artillery cannot be given a new crew if it is being crewed by another unit. If the original crew is still on the battlefield, it must first take an Assignment action to abandon some or all of the Artillery, or the crew must be at least 12" away from their guns at the end of an activation. Then another unit may be assigned to the abandoned Artillery.

Any unit can crew any abandoned Artillery, no matter which force originally fielded it. If any unit is Cohesive with one or more abandoned Artillery pieces at the start of an activation, they may use an Assignment action to do so.

To continue the example above, the unit of 4 models assigned to the 4 Light Cannons takes 2 Casualties. Another unit of 6 models is moved into the same deck section as the gun crew and its Cannons.

When the gun crew is activated, it takes an Assignment action to abandon three of its Cannons (2 larboard and 1 starboard), leaving it with only 1 of its original guns. Later in the turn, the unit of 6 models activates, and takes and Assignment action to crew the 3 Light Cannons that the original crew had abandoned.

7.3 Reloading Artillery

A unit may simultaneously reload as many Artillery pieces as it can effectively crew.

For example, a unit of 6 models is crewing 2 Medium Cannons, which have a minimum crew requirement of 3 models each. The unit can use one Reload Action to remove Reload markers from both guns simultaneously, since it has met the minimum crew requirement for both guns.

If a unit cannot meet the minimum crew requirements for all Artillery they are Reloading, the unit may only Reload as many Artillery pieces as they can effectively crew.

Continuing the example above, the unit of 6 takes 2 Casualties. They do not have enough models remaining in the unit to crew both Medium Cannons effectively. They must ignore Reloading one of the guns to meet the minimum crew requirement in order to Reload the other one.

Artillery crewed at its minimum requirement or greater Reloads at the normal rate; one Reload action (taken as a Standard action) removes one Reload marker.

Artillery crewed at less than its minimum requirement Reloads as a Dedicated action: remove 1 Reload marker per activation regardless of how many actions are spent. Remember that suit-activated Special Rules (like Artillery Crew) won't trigger when Reloading as a Dedicated action.

7.4 Moving Artillery

Artillery in Structures cannot be moved unless dictated by a scenario.

Artillery on a field carriage (Swivels, Light and Medium Cannons) can be moved, but cannot be fired if they moved earlier in the same activation. A Heavy Cannon on a field carriage cannot be moved at all.

» Moving an Artillery piece on a field carriage reduces a unit's Move distance in addition to any Rough terrain the unit might be moving through (see Artillery Stats below). The crew must meet the minimum crew requirement to move a gun; with less than the minimum crew, it can only pivot.

» A gun's crew may not climb with an Artillery piece on a field carriage. Likewise, a gun on a field carriage cannot be "picked up" or pulled across object terrain that is 1" or taller.

» A gun on a field carriage may be moved into a Structure, but only if it has a door (not window) large enough to roll it through.

Artillery pieces are objects that can provide Cover to models. This is less relevant when a gun is mounted in a Structure, but much more relevant when mounted on a field carriage.

7.5 Destroying Artillery

Artillery that is in a Structure section can only be destroyed with Critical Damage. (See Critical Hits and Lucky Hits below.)

Artillery on field carriages cannot be targeted by Small Arms and Swivels, but count as models in the unit if that unit is attacked by Cannons. This means Artillery pieces on field carriages can (and must) be removed as Casualties if successfully hit by a Cannon. Artillery pieces on field carriages always receive a standard 6+ Ranged Save when in Cover.

Any unit that is crewing Artillery, or is within 1" of any abandoned Artillery has the option to spike the guns so they may not fall into enemy hands in the future (see Spike Artillery under Actions). A spiked Cannon cannot be fired for the rest of the game, but it remains on the battlefield until it is destroyed completely by some other means.

7.6 Making a Ranged Attack with Artillery

Note: When Charged, Artillery Crews can make Defensive Attacks with the weapons they are carrying, not the Artillery they are crewing (unless it is a Swivel gun).

1. CHOOSE A TARGET.

Choose an enemy unit that isn't in a Structure or a Structure section to be the target of the Ranged Attack. Enemy units cannot be targeted inside a Structure.

2. CHECK LINE OF SIGHT.

Check to see that each Artillery piece in the attacking unit has Line of Sight to a least one model in the target unit or to the target Structure section. Only those models or sections can be targeted for the Shoot Test in Step 5.

Artillery has a limited Arc of Fire, which may affect drawing a Line of Sight.

» The Arc of Fire for a Cannon on a ship is the width of the deck it is on (this will be explained fully in the upcoming Ships section).

» The Arc of Fire for a Cannon on a fortification is a pivot of up to 45° from its current facing, after which the gun may fire. If it pivots farther than this, it counts as a movement, and the gun may not fire.

» The Arc of Fire for a gun on a field carriage is a pivot of up to 45° from its current facing, after which the gun may fire. If it pivots farther than this, it counts as a movement, and the gun may not fire.

The ship turning gauge is also useful for determining the Arc of Fire for Artillery on field carriages or on fortifications. Line up the Wind Direction arrow pointed down the center line of an Artillery piece, and the line separating Windward and In the Winds Eye is as far as the gun can pivot and still fire.

If no model or Artillery piece in the shooting unit has Line of Sight to the target unit, that unit may not be targeted. The shooting unit may select a different enemy unit as long as Line of Sight can be drawn between it.

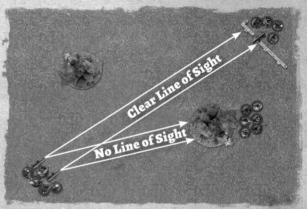

Figure 47

In Figure 47, the unit to the left wants to shoot its Cannons at the enemy. The stand of trees blocks Line of Sight to the unit behind it, so the attacking unit decides to target an enemy unit that has a Cannon set up in a ruin.

3. CHOOSE A WEAPON TO FIRE.

If the unit is making a Ranged Attack with one or more Artillery, each Artillery piece must have 0 Reload markers in order to be fired. The controlling player declares what eligible Artillery pieces it will fire.

Artillery cannot be fired if the unit crewing it moved or participated in a Melee Combat earlier in the activation. Likewise, an Artillery piece cannot fire if it moved earlier in the same activation. Pivoting a gun (as described in step 2) does not count as a movement.

A unit may make a Ranged Attack with Small Arms or Artillery, but never both in the same Activation.

In the example above, both of the Cannon in the attacking unit (one light and one medium) have 0 Reload markers, so the unit opts to fire with both.

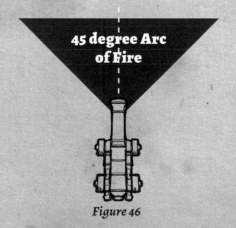

Figure 46

4. CHECK DISTANCE TO TARGET.

Measure the distance between the firing unit and the target unit (*see Measuring Distances p.31*).
Unless otherwise noted, all Shoot Tests receive a +1 penalty for every 4" between the target unit and the shooting unit.

Range	0" to <4"	4" to <8"	8" to <12"	12" to <16"	16" to <20"	20" to <24"	24" to <28"	28" to <32"	32" to <36"
Modifier	+0	+1	+2	+3	+4	+5	+6	+7	+8

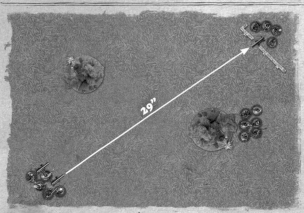

Figure 48

In Figure 48, the closest Cannon in the attacking unit is 29" from the unit in the ruin. This imposes a +7 penalty to the Shoot Test.

5. ROLL THE SHOOT TEST.

The attacker will roll one d10 per Cannon attempting the Shoot Test, regardless of the type of Cannon being fired. Swivel guns roll 3 d10 for each Swivel being fired.

The unit making the Ranged Attack spends 1 Action, and rolls the appropriate number of dice.

> » If all Artillery being fired are the same type, all dice may be rolled together. If not, roll for each gun individually, or use different colored dice for each type

The first Shoot Test attempted by a unit during their activation is made without consequence. For every additional Shoot Test that unit attempts during their activation, the unit gains 1 Fatigue point.

When Cannons are fired they have a base target number of 0 (NOT the unit's Shoot skill), modified by the range, to determine hits. Swivel Guns have a base target number of 6.

Each roll that is equal to or greater than the target number (base target number + range modifier) counts as a hit on the targeted unit.

To continue the example above, the attacking unit rolls 2 dice because they are attacking with two Cannon. The target number to hit is 7 (0 base + 7 range penalty = 7+). Both dice are rolled. The results on the dice are 7 and 9, so both guns scored a hit on the unit.

The rolls for the Artillery Shoot Test to determine the initial hits are separate from the dice rolled to score additional hits. This means that a reroll for the Shoot Test (like spending a Fortune Point) could reroll the initial Shoot Test results or the additional hits results, but not both.

6. ADD RELOAD MARKERS.

When a Cannon is fired, it gains 4 Reload markers. A Swivel Gun gains 2.

Both Cannons in the example above gain 4 Reload markers.

7. OPPOSING PLAYER ROLLS RANGED SAVES AND REMOVES CASUALTIES.

The defending unit may attempt one Ranged Save per model in the unit, but cannot attempt more Saves than hits taken.

The defending unit's Ranged Save value will differ when models are in and out of Cover. See Terrain and Ranged Combat (*p. 55*) for exact details about determining Cover, but put simply:

> » Count the models in Cover first, and assign an equal number of hits to be saved using their Ranged Save values first. The target number of the Ranged Save of a model in Cover is the defending unit's Shoot Save value.

> » If any hits remain unassigned and there are models in the defending unit that are not in Cover, then apply a Ranged Save value of 9+ to each remaining hit for each model that is not in Cover.

Roll one d10 per Save being attempted, following the criteria above. If a unit is attempting Saves with different target numbers, either roll the Saves separately, or roll different colored dice for each to differentiate them. Each roll that equals or exceeds the target number cancels 1 hit.

Subtract the number of successful Saves from the number of hits taken. Any remaining hits are removed as Casualties, at the discretion of the defending player.

The defending unit in the example above has taken 5 hits. The unit has a Shoot skill of (7/8), and the unit has all its models in Hard Cover. 4 d10 are rolled for the Ranged Saves, with a target number of 7+ (Shoot Save of 8 -1 bonus for Hard Cover =7+). The results rolled are 1, 4, 7, 7. Two Saves are made.

5 hits – 2 successful Saves = the unit removes 3 models as Casualties.

8. DEFENDING UNIT ROLLS A FATIGUE TEST.

If the targeted unit took hits (even if it suffered no Casualties) it must take a Fatigue Test, and may gain Fatigue as a result (see Fatigue Test).

7.7 *Firing Artillery at Structures*

HITTING AND DAMAGING STRUCTURES

All Structures have a Fortitude and Integrity rating to reflect their durability in the face of heavy fire.

A structure's Fortitude is a measure of how difficult it is for Artillery to damage the structure. The Structure's Fortitude gives a penalty to any incoming Artillery Shoot Test.

A battery of 3 Light Cannons are firing on a ship with a Fortitude of 3 and an Integrity of 4. The ship is 15" away from the guns. The cannons need a 6 to hit (0 base, +3 for the range, +3 for the ship's Fortitude.)

When firing Artillery at a Structure, each successful hit results in a point of damage to the Structure. Mark off the appropriate number of boxes on the Structure's card, or keep track on a piece of paper.

A Structure's Integrity value is the amount of damage a Structure can take before it's Fortitude is reduced.

When damage taken equals or exceeds the Structure's Integrity value, the Structure's Fortitude is permanently reduced by one. The reduction takes effect immediately after all damage from an attack is resolved.

Continuing the example above, 3 d10 are rolled for the Shoot Test, with the following results: 1, 8, 8. Two of the 3 Light Cannons hit. Additional dice are rolled for the guns that hit (+2 for each Light Cannon), with the results of 2, 3, 7, 8. Added up, the ship takes 4 hits (4 points of damage).

The ship had 2 points of damage from a previous attack, the ship's owner ticks off an additional 4 boxes of damage on the ship card. The ship accumulated damage equal to or greater than its Integrity of 4, thereby reducing the ship's Fortitude from 3 to 2.

A Structure can never go below 1 Fortitude.

Type	Fortitude	Integrity
Shanty	1	1
Wooden Building	1	2
Large Wooden Building	2	2
Stone Building	2	2
Large Stone Building	2	3
Very Large Building (Any Type)	3	3

Table 3: Fortitude on Integrity of common buildings

ARTILLERY HITS AGAINST UNITS IN STRUCTURES

For each point of damage that a Structure takes, a model within the Structure might also be removed as a casualty. Each hit must be applied to units within the section of the Structure that was targeted. If there are no units in the section that the Artillery fired upon, no hits are applied to units.

For example, if a section of a building takes 3 hits from Artillery fire, the unit in that section would take 3 hits as well.

All hits are distributed as evenly as possible among all units in the affected section, as explained in Structures (p. 67). Once all hits are distributed, each struck unit takes the appropriate Saves, removes Casualties, and tests for Fatigue as usual.

For example, if a section of a ship containing 2 units takes 5 hits, one unit would take 3 hits, the other would take 2 (which units take which hits would be decided by the controlling player).

Hits to units in or below a ship's Rigging are handled a little differently, and are explained in the Targeting Ships section (p. 90).

DESTROYING STRUCTURES

Structures are not destroyed by normal damage; they are only destroyed by Critical Damage. There are two methods for inflicting Critical Damage on a Structure:

Lucky Hits: If a player rolls at least one natural 10 for the Shoot Test of an Artillery attack against a Structure, roll once (and only once) on the Critical Damage Table for the appropriate Structure type. Subtract one from the roll, and determine the final result.

For example, a fortification has been hit once by Artillery fire, but the result rolled was a 10. The fortification takes 1 point of damage, and the attacking player rolls a d10 on the Fortification Critical Damage Table. The result is a 6. After subtracting one from the roll (6 - 1 = 5), the final result is determined to be Debris.

If for some reason a Lucky Hit causes you to roll on another

Critical Damage table, subtract one from that roll as well.

Critical Hits: If an Artillery attack inflicts a number of hits that are equal to (or greater than) twice the current Fortitude value of the Structure being fired upon (after all damage from the attack has been applied), roll once on the Critical Damage Table for the appropriate Structure type. Roll once on the table for each time you double the Structure's Fortitude.

For example, a shanty with a Fortitude of 1 is hit 6 times by an Artillery attack from a ship. This attack doubles the shack's For-titude three times, therefore three d10 are rolled on the Building Critical Damage Table.

A Structure may take only one Lucky Hit, but any number of additional Critical Hits may be scored if the damage conditions are met.

For example, a ship is hit 6 times, and two of the results rolled were natural 10s. After all damage is applied, the ship's Fortitude value is 2. This would result in one Lucky Hit (because you can only score one, no matter how many natural 10s are rolled), and the ship takes an additional Critical Hits (because the damage to the ship doubled its current Fortitude once).

The Critical Damage tables for each Structure type can be found in the Structure section of the rules.

7.8 Ranged Weapons: Artillery

Table 4: *Artillery Stats Chart*

GUN TYPE	MINIMUM CREW	D10 ROLLED PER GUN	SHOOT TEST BASE NUMBER	RELOAD MARKERS GAINED AFTER FIRING	ARC OF FIRE ON SHIP	ARC OF FIRE ON FIELD CARRIAGE OR FORTIFICA-TION	MOVE PENALTY ON FIELD CARRIAGE	POINTS PER GUN (ON A STRUCTURE)	POINTS PER GUN (ON A FIELD CARRIAGE)
Swivel Gun	2	3 vs. Units & Rigging only	6	2	360°	360°	-1"	2	4
Light Cannon	2	1 (+2)	0	4	Width of deck	45° pivot	-1"	5	10
Medium Cannon	3	1 (+3)	0	4	Width of deck	45° pivot	-2"	7	14
Heavy Cannon	4	1 (+4)	0	4	Width of deck	45° pivot	immobile	9	18

* Cannons on ships are purchased in pairs.

The Point values listed include Artillery when building a force. *(See Creating a Force. p. 94)*

CANNONS

All Cannons (not Swivels) have the following traits:

> » Exceptional Range: if the target number of a Shoot Test made with this weapon is any number 11 or greater, the Shoot Test can be attempted, and will succeed on a natural 10.

A single natural 10 does not score a Lucky hit when the target number to hit is 11+. Two or more results must be natural 10s to score a Lucky hit.

For example, a single Light Cannon from a gun carriage is shooting at a ship in a harbor. Due to the distance and the ship's Fortitude, the Cannon crew needs a 13 to hit the ship. But due to the exceptional range of Cannons, hits can still be scored on any roll of Natural 10.

The Shoot Test for the Light Cannon is rolled, and hits with a 10. Since it hit, two more dice are rolled, with results of 3 and 8. One hit is scored, but no Lucky hit (a Lucky hit would have been scored if at least two results were natural 10s).

> » Lethal to unprotected units: If a unit that is not in a Structure is the target of a Ranged Attack from Artillery, there is a chance extra hits will be inflicted on the unit. As such, any natural 10 rolled for the Artillery Shoot Test will count as 2 hits against an unprotected unit.

SWIVEL GUNS

A Swivel is a lightweight Artillery piece designed primarily for anti-personnel use. As such, it blurs the line between Artillery and Small Arms.

> » Swivels are crewed and Reloaded as Artillery.

> » Swivels have a base target number of 6+ for Shoot Tests.

> » Units with Artillery-related special rules (like Artillery Crew) may apply them to Swivels, but not special rules that would apply to Small Arms (like Fast Reload).

> » Swivels have a 360° Arc of Fire to represent their lighter weight and mobility (they can be moved to another part of the section and be braced on a gunwale or window sill, for example). However, they cannot be removed from the Structure section to which they were placed when purchased.

> » Swivels target units in the manner of Small Arms, not Artillery. Therefore, Swivels may only target units, units inside Structures, and ship's Rigging.

> » Swivels can be used to make Defensive Attacks when charged.

Huzzah! You've done it again! You've reach a point where you should really stop reading the rules and play a game! The ship section will go much smoother once you've tried your hand at some combat involving Structures and Artillery.

After you find an opponent (maybe the same one as last time), skip down to the Creating a Force section, and make another small force of around 100 points per player. Don't worry about the specifics of buying Artillery for units, simply take one Light Cannon per force (or find a suitable proxy) and assign it to one unit in each force. The assigned unit doesn't even need any Artillery skills.

Set up an all-land game board just like last time ... around 3'x3', or maybe a little wider, with a lot of terrain on the table. But this time, mix in a Structure or two, evenly spaced along the centerline of the game board. If you don't have any structures in your terrain collection, don't worry. If you have a utility knife, a marker, and a small box from your favorite online mail order megacorporation, you can whip up a serviceable proxy building in about five minutes!

Once that is complete, set up and play the Land version of the Take and Hold scenario. After a game or two, you should have a good grasp on this block of rules. Then it's on to the Ship rules! (Finally!)

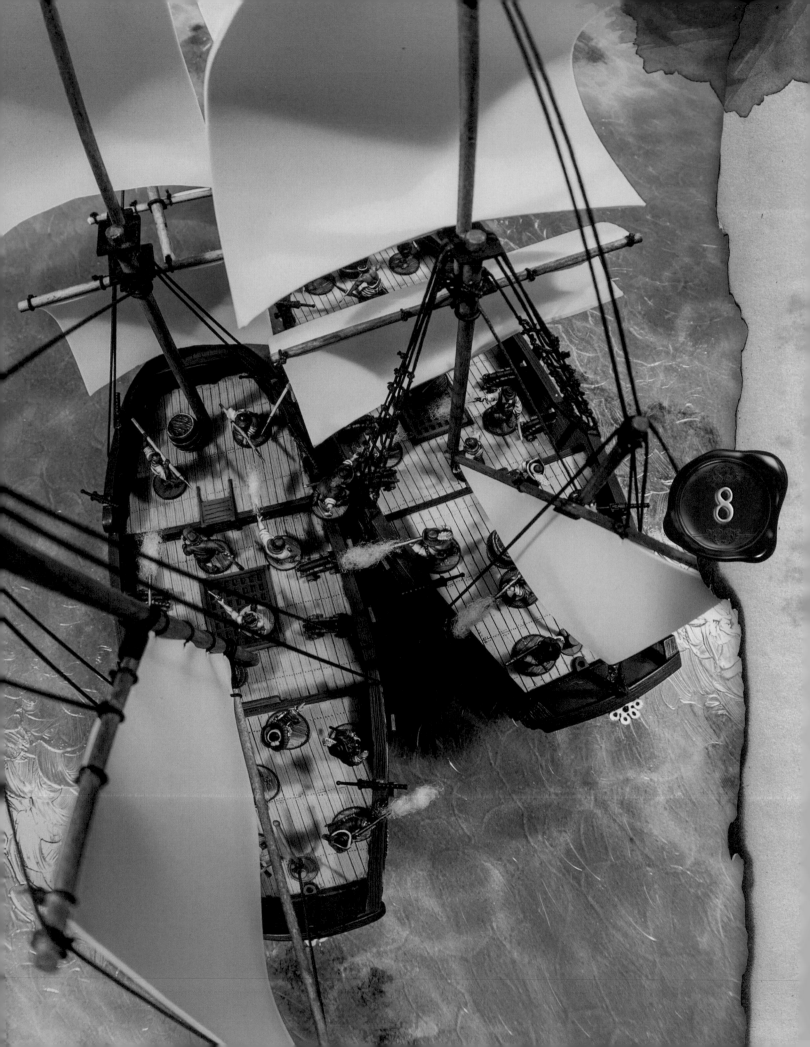

8
Ships

hips in Blood & Plunder are treated like Structures. In game terms, they are essentially fortifications that can move through Deep and Shoal water terrain. All ships obey the standard rules for Structures outlined in the Structures section (*p. 64*) unless they are modified by the rules to follow.

A ship is a Structure that is actually two separate Structures (the Hull and the Rigging) joined together.

» The ship's **Hull** is the body of the ship upon which sits the weather deck and super-structure. The bulk of the crew and all of the Artillery are placed here. Sections in the Hull are called **decks**. Damage to the decks will kill the crew and potentially destroy the ship. Ship decks are almost always open-topped.

» A ship's **Rigging** is the collection of masts and sails connected to the Hull that moves the ship. Sections of the Rigging are known as **masts**. Damage to the rigging will cripple the ship's movement but will not sink the ship, and is less lethal to the crew. Units cannot occupy the masts unless the ship has the Fighting Top trait.

The Rigging is divided into sections, equal in number and location to the decks of the ship it is part of. (so measurements to a mast are the same as measuring to a deck section).

A **boat** is a type of ship that is smaller in size. All boats only have a single Hull deck, and the Rigging is smaller and not treated as a separate structure (hence cannot be targeted separately). Any rules specific to boats can found at the end of the ship rules.

This book contains game stats for some of the most common vessels found in the Caribbean during the 17th century. These include:

» **Sloop:** Sloops are small swift vessels which sail well to windward and can venture close to shore. These fore and aft rigged ships were preferred among smugglers and coastal raiders.

» **Brigantine:** Quick, sturdy and well-armed, the brigantine is suited to handle nearly any situation. This ship's shallow draft and mixed rig configuration gives it a versatility which made it very popular among Pirate and Privateer crews.

» **Light Frigate:** These light warships were made for combat and Commonly used by the Guarda Costas and pirate hunters. Light Frigates are robust vessels which are designed to mimic their larger counter parts while keeping up with the smaller ships they pursued.

» **Longboat:** These open boats where used primarily to move from ship to shore and back again. They where on occasion used in small "fleets" by Pirates and Privateers to take on larger ships as well.

Game Stats for these ships can be found on page 121.

8.1 *Ship Characteristics*

Each ship in the game has a number of characteristics that describe its abilities. This information is listed on every Ship Card and is explained below:

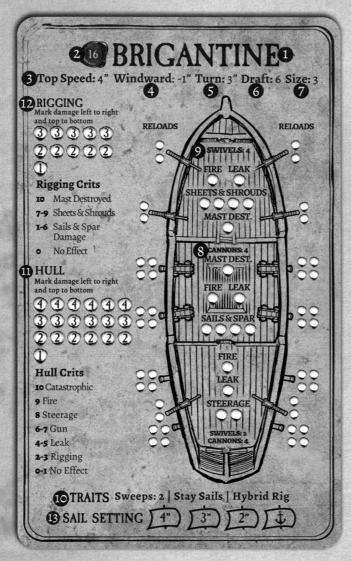

Figure 49: An example of a ship's card

① **SHIP TYPE**

② **POINTS:** The number of points that must be spent to add the ship to your force. *(See Building a Force. p. 94)*

③ **TOP SPEED:** The ship's maximum speed.

④ **WINDWARD:** The amount of speed lost when sailing into the wind.

⑤ **TURN:** The maximum number of inches that may be moved while making a turn. Higher numbers mean a ship is more maneuverable.

⑥ **DRAFT:** How much of a ship's hull dips below the waterline. A high value means your ship is more likely to Run Aground in Shoals.

⑦ **SIZE:** The number of sections (decks) the ship has.

⑧ **CANNONS:** The total number of Cannons a ship can carry. These are broken down by deck.

⑨ **SWIVELS:** The maximum number of Swivels a ship can carry. These are also broken down by deck.

⑩ **TRAITS:** Any special rules the ship may have.

⑪ **HULL FORTITUDE & INTEGRITY:** The printed number on each bubble represents the ship's current fortitude. Each column represents its integrity.

⑫ **RIGGING FORTITUDE & INTEGRITY:** The printed number on each bubble represents the ship's current fortitude. Each column represents its integrity.

⑬ **SAIL SETTING:** The ship's available speed settings when moving under sail.

8.2 *Ship Movement*

Ships are in constant motion, unless they are immobile for some reason. To represent this, a ship that is able to move at the start of a turn will always move 3 times during a turn during a unit's activation.

A ship will move via wind-driven movement under sail, being rowed with Sweeps, or passively Drifting. These means of movement and how far a ship will move is explained in the next section.

All ships in a player's force must move:

» any time during the first activation of that player's turn.

» any time during the last activation of that player's turn.

» any time during one activation in between the first and last of that player's turn, at the discretion of the controlling player.

Movements can be made at any time during the activation, even in between unit actions, but cannot be moved in the middle of an action. Ships may not move more than once during an activation, unless noted by a ship Trait.

A ship movement does not require the activated unit to spend actions to move the ship if it is making a Basic Maneuver, like moving forward and executing turns (*see Basic Maneuvers p. 85*).

If a ship has any of its 3 moves left at the end of the turn (usually because a force doesn't have 3 units to activate), the ship will move on its own at the end of the turn (*see Residual Ship Movement below*).

CIRCUMSTANCES THAT REDUCE SHIP MOVEMENT

At times, ships will become mobile later in a turn, like ships that pull up anchor and empty boats that are boarded and launched.

When this occurs, simply pick up movement for the ship at the appropriate point, following the criteria for ship movement above as closely as you can.

For example, a force with 4 units pulls up anchor on the second activation of a turn. Since the ship couldn't move during the first activation, that movement is ignored. The ship only needs to move during the last activation, and an activation in-between (at that player's discretion).

In another example, if a boat launches from a ship during the last activation of a turn, it only has to move once (for that last activation). The other two movements are ignored because the boat was not able to move at the appropriate times.

RESIDUAL SHIP MOVEMENT

If a ship has unused movement actions at the end of a turn, the ship must take them.

» If moving under sail or being rowed with Sweeps, any ship with residual movement must move once at its current speed for each movement it did not take. Normal turning is allowed, but a ship may not change Sail Settings or attempt an Advanced Maneuver. Each unused movement is measured and resolved separately.

» If a ship with residual movement is In the Wind's Eye, at 0" Sail Setting, or is otherwise immobile, it drifts at the mercy of the wind and sea.

If multiple ships in any force have residual movement, the ship with the highest current speed moves first and resolves all unused movement. If there is a tie, roll a single d10 for each tied ship. The ship with the highest roll moves first.

8.3 *Moving Under Sail*

A ship under sail will always move at its:

SAIL SETTING +/- WIND – RIGGING CRITICAL DAMAGE

The distance that a ship moves is determined right before the movement is taken, using the criteria as explained below. The ship must move this distance, and cannot move less.

1. SAIL SETTING

A ship's Sail Setting is an abstract representation of how much sail the ship is using to maintain a certain speed.

The Sail Setting must be chosen and marked on the ship card at the beginning of the game, and may not be changed unless a unit aboard the ship takes a Dedicated action to do so. A Sail Setting cannot be changed by a unit if there is an enemy unit on the same ship.

The target number for the test to change the Sail Setting is 7+ (or 5+ if the unit has the Sailors Special Rule). If the test is failed, the sails stay at the current setting and no further negative effect is applied.

The ship's Sail Setting may only be moved up or down one speed value per activation. A new sail setting takes effect immediately.

A ship with its sails set to 0" will still drift unless it is immobile for some other reason. A ship that is Anchored (at its lowest Sail Setting) cannot move or drift until it is no longer anchored.

2. WIND

The direction from which the wind is blowing, the wind speed, and your ship's relative position are all important for determining how wind affects a ship's speed.

◊ WIND DIRECTION AND SPEED

The wind always blows across the table from one of the four table edges, and is determined by the Scenario or at random before the game begins. The wind will always be blowing from the selected table edge unless changed by an Event card (*see Events p. 128*).

Wind speed is measured in strength from -2 (very little wind) to +2 (a gale). A ship's total inches moved will be increased or decreased by this number. The default wind speed is always assumed to be +/- 0 unless a Scenario dictates otherwise or an Event changes it.

The wind speed is applied to every ship movement made under sail, no matter the circumstances.

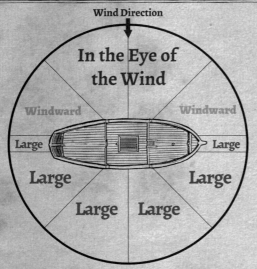

Figure 50: *An illustrated representation of Point of Sail*

◊ POINT OF SAIL

A ship's Point of Sail is its position in relation to the wind direction. To determine a ship's Point of Sail, first determine if the wind is off the ship's bow or stern, or if the wind is abeam (directly on the side).

» The wind is off the stern if the rear end of the ship is closer to the edge of the table from which the wind is blowing. If the wind is hitting the ship directly on the side, the wind is abeam.

If the wind is abeam or off the stern, the ship is sailing Large. The ship travels its current Sail Setting speed.

» The wind is off the bow if the front end of the ship is closer than the stern to the edge of the table from which the wind is blowing. If this is the case, the ship is sailing Windward. A ship sailing Windward applies the Windward movement penalty listed on the ship's unit card to its current Sail Setting speed.

» A ship under sail may not move forward while its bow is pointing closer than 45° to the wind. If a ship starts an activation with its bow within 45° of the wind and attempts to take a Basic Maneuver, it has lost forward momentum and is immediately In the Wind's Eye. Only an Advanced Maneuver (*p. 86*) can make a ship move forward while it is closer than 45° to the wind.

A ship caught In the Wind's Eye is considered to be Drifting. (*See Drifting p. 84.*) It will continue to drift each time it takes a movement, until it begins an activation with its bow pointed more than 45° away from the wind.

Figure 51 shows how the turning gauge is used to determine if a ship is too close to the wind.

» Place the bow of the ship in the cut out corner of the turning gauge.

» Line the marked edge of the gauge with the wind direction as indicated.

» If the ship's bowline in inside (not on) the dotted line, it's In the Wind's Eye.

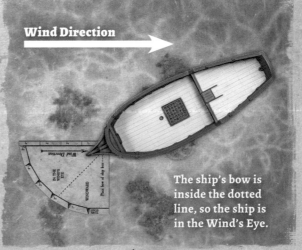

The ship's bow is inside the dotted line, so the ship is in the Wind's Eye.

Figure 51

3. RIGGING CRITICAL DAMAGE

All Rigging Critical Damage has a negative effect on a ship movement. This is explained on the Ship Rigging Critical Damage table in the Structures section.

EXCEEDING TOP SPEED

Whenever a ship is forced to move faster than its Top Speed value, it will damage its Rigging.

When this happens, the ship will move only as far as its Top Speed; any additional movement is lost. Each 1" of movement the ship would have moved in excess of its Top Speed applied as a Lucky Hit to the Rigging.

For example, a ship with a Top Speed of 4" has its Sail Setting at 4" and is sailing Large. An Event card changes the wind speed from 0 to +1. The player chooses to move the ship on the next activation. The ship is ready to move 5" (4" for the Sail Setting +1" for the wind), but can only move 4" as limited by its Top Speed. As a result, the ship moves 4", and the player rolls a Lucky Hit on the Ship Rigging Critical Damage table.

MOVING UNDER OARS (SWEEPS)

Ships with the Sweeps trait have the option to move under oar power instead of sails. To move under oars:

» The ship must have its Sail Setting at 0".

» An active unit in the middlemost section of the ship takes an Assignment action to crew the Sweeps. Once this action is taken, the unit is powering the ship's movement until its next activation, and it cannot take any actions aside from Rally.

» As long as the unit on the Sweeps does not become Shaken, the ship may make movements normally (3 times a turn, as described under Ship Movement above). Otherwise, the ship will drift.

» The size of the unit on the Sweeps determines how far the ship can move. For all ships:

• If the rowing unit has at least 2 models in it for every deck the ship has, the ship moves at its full Sweeps value

• If the rowing unit has at least 1 model in it for every deck the ship has, the ship moves at half its Sweeps value

• If the rowing unit has fewer models in it than the ship has decks, then the ship cannot move under oars at all.

» The next time that the unit crewing the Sweeps activates, they have the option of taking an Assignment action to abandon the Sweeps. If not, the unit stays on the Sweeps until the next time it is activated. If a unit assigned to the Sweeps is Charged, they automatically abandon the Sweeps and may attempt Melee Saves if necessary.

A ship being rowed is not affected by the wind and may move in any direction (including backward), but still executes turns as described below under Turning. No Advanced Maneuvers can be attempted when moving under oars.

A ship under Sweeps does not need to move its full move distance whenever it makes a movement, but if it doesn't move at least 1" it will drift instead.

DRIFTING

Drifting is usually a detriment. The player has no control over the movement of their ship and it does not move very far. This may make the ship a sitting duck, although it can be used for tactical advantage at times.

If a ship must drift, it moves to turn its bow away from the wind direction, moving at the current wind speed +1". An example Drifting is found below under Turning.

If the ship's point of sail was windward, this will result in a backward turn. If not, the drift results in a forward turn. Turns are made following the Turning rules explained below

Drifting occurs at the same time as normal ship movement, and unused Drift movements apply to residual ship movement at the end of the turn.

SHIPS MOVING BACKWARDS

In any situation where a ship is moving backward (no matter the circumstances), the maximum movement distance is 3".

8.4 Ship Maneuvers
BASIC MANEUVERS

These are simple maneuvers that ships can make without requiring any unit to spend an action.

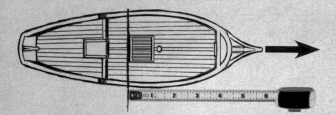 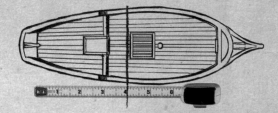

Figure 52: A Sloop moves 4" straight forward

◊ MOVE FORWARD

The simplest (and most common) basic maneuver is to sail forward a distance equal to your current speed (as determined above)*(see Figure 52)*.

Remember, a ship must move the full value of its current speed, up to its Top Speed; you cannot stop short.

Turns may be made at the beginning or end of your forward movement. *(See Turning below.)*

◊ TURNING

A ship may Turn up to its maximum Turn value each time it moves. Any distance spent on turning is subtracted from the ship's total for that movement.

Use the provided turning gauge to measure the distance and arc of the turn *(see Figure 53)*.

To make a turn:

» Place the gauge flat against the same side of the

ship as the direction you wish to turn, and line up the Start arrow with a point on the side about half way down the vessel.

All ships produced by Firelock Games will have skids or hanging ropes along the sides to make lining up the Start arrow easier. If you do not have one of our ships (which is a shame really, because our ships are pretty fantastic!), be sure to place the gauge at the same point when turning.

» Move your ship along the gauge the desired number of inches by lining up your reference point with the appropriate arrow. Make sure that the ship is flat against the gauge when finished turning.

A ship with no models on its rearmost deck suffers a -1" penalty to all turns unless it is drifting.

A turning maneuver must be made at the beginning or the end of the ship's movement.

If a ship is required to make a backward Turn, flip the turning gauge upside down and measure it as described above.

 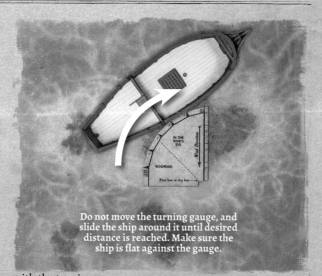

Line up Start arrow with the skids on the side of the ship.

Do not move the turning gauge, and slide the ship around it until desired distance is reached. Make sure the ship is flat against the gauge.

Figure 53: Executing a 4" Turn with the turning gauge

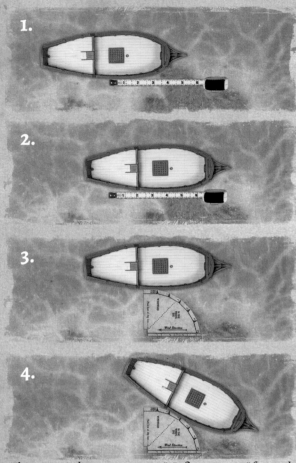

Figure 54: *A sloop must move 4". It first moves 2" forward, then executes a 2" turn at the end of its move (totaling 4")*

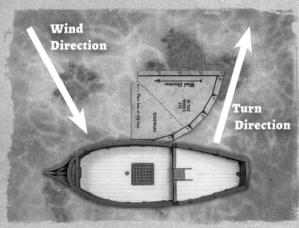

Figure 55

The ship in Figure 55 is drifting, and will have to make a backward turn away from the wind.

ADVANCED MANEUVERS

These tricky maneuvers involve an element of risk, but can be decisive in battle.

Attempting an advanced maneuver requires a unit on board to take a Dedicated action. An Advanced Maneuver cannot be attempted by a unit if there is an enemy unit on the same ship.

The target number for the Test is 7+ (or 5+ if the unit has the Sailors special rule). If successful, immediately perform the maneuver as described below. If failed, the maneuver does not occur, and a negative effect may be applied.

◊ BOX HAULING

Box Hauling allows a ship that begins an activation within 45° of the wind to sail backward. A ship that Box Hauls will move backward at its current sail setting or 3", whichever is less. Backward Turns may be made while Box Hauling.

If the attempt to Box Haul fails, the ship is immediately In the Wind's Eye and drifts. Also roll and apply a Lucky Hit to the ship's Rigging.

◊ TACKING

Tacking allows a ship that begins an activation within 45° of the wind to attempt a forward Turn into the wind. A ship that tacks must use all available movement or 3" to Turn, whichever is less. The ship may not exceed its Turn value.

If an attempt to tack fails, the ship is immediately In the Wind's Eye and drifts. Also roll and apply a Lucky Hit to the ship's Rigging.

◊ WEARING

A Wearing maneuver allows a ship to add +1 to its Turn value when turning away from the wind. You cannot turn farther than your ship's current speed.

If the attempt at Wearing fails, the ship may still turn its normal Turn value.

If a ship within 45° of the wind at the end of a Wearing maneuver (whether or not it was successful), roll and apply a Lucky Hit to the ship's Rigging.

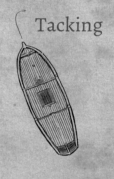

Wind Direction

Box Hauling

Tacking

Wearing

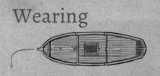

Figure 56: *Advanced Maneuvers*

8.5 Unfortunate Consequences of Ship Movement

SAILING OFF THE TABLE

Ships may never sail off the table to leave a battle (unless the Scenario dictates otherwise). If a ship were ever forced to do so, players must "scroll" the map to keep all ships on the table.

To scroll the map, measure a distance and a direction that would place all ships back near the center of the table. Move all ships this distance and direction, being careful not to change their orientation. Terrain on the map should be repositioned using the same method (*see Figure 57*).

If scrolling causes any terrain to be moved off the table, the player whose ship did not sail off the table may reposition the terrain along the "new" edge of the table, at least 10" away from any ships

If there is a lot of terrain on the table, then ships may have to be repositioned much closer to the edges so there is enough room to legally place all the terrain back on the board.

If scrolling would:

» force another player's ship off the table, or

» force off a land mass that includes game elements like units or objectives, or

» any other scrolling-related conflict,

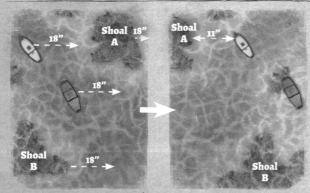

Figure 57

In Figure 57, the active ship is about to sail off the map, causing the map to scroll. Both players decide that 18" straight across the table will work, so all ships and terrain elements move 18" right.

This 18" scroll moves Shoal A off the table. The player that is not causing the scroll places Shoal A along the "new" table edge, 11" away from the red player's ship. The placement is intended to hinder the red player's turning options...

then the ship that is currently sailing off the map suddenly hits an unseen Shoal and Runs Aground (*see below*). (Cowardice and rules exploitation will not be tolerated in Blood & Plunder!)

RUNNING AGROUND

Any time a ship with a Draft value ends its movement within an area of Shoal terrain, there is a chance it will Run Aground.

To see if a ship has Run Aground, roll one D10 and add the ship's Draft value to the roll.

1–14	No effect.
15+	The ship has Run Aground hard. It takes D5 Hull damage. (Units on the ship are unaffected.)

If a ship Runs Aground it becomes immobile, will not drift, and may not move unless freed.

To free a ship:

» the ship must first reduce its sail setting to 0", then make a successful Repair Action.

» Once the Repair Action is successful, the ship immediately moves 3" backward (turning is allowed). This counts as one of the ship's 3 movements for the Turn.

COLLISIONS

◊ SHIP TO SHIP

When ships collide, both ships may take damage to their Rigging and/or become fouled (stuck together).

A collision only occurs if a ship sails bow-first or stern-first into another ship (*see Figure 58*). When a collision occurs, the ship that caused the collision stops moving, even if it did not move its full distance that movement. The collision is then resolved as described below.

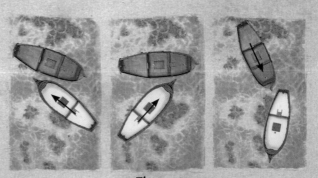

Figure 58

When a collision occurs, the active player rolls a d10 and references the chart below:

1–5	Hulls collide
6–9	Rigging collides
10	Rigging Collides and ships are fouled.

Both ships take damage when struck. Each ship takes damage equal to the size of the other ship minus one. Damage is applied to the location rolled on the chart above at the point of impact. Units in either ship are unaffected.

If the ship causing the collision was drifting, roll on the table above. But do not apply damage to either ship.

If two ships collide and do not become fouled, the struck ship is moved 3" **directly away** from the ship that struck it.

To move a ship "directly away" from something, slide the ship away from the point where they are touching as if the ships pushed off of each other, but do not turn the ships at all *(see Figure 59)*. If this is not possible for some reason, the other ship is moved away instead.

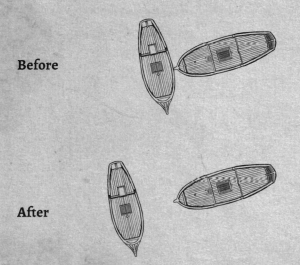

Before

After

Figure 59: The ship is moved directly away from a ship that collided with it.

If the ships become fouled, they are considered to be connected at the point of impact and are treated as a single Structure that is drifting. This is explained fully under Throwing and Releasing Grapples below.

Ships may be unfouled with a successful Repair Action. When the two ships are no longer joined together, the ship that made the Repair action is moved 3" directly away from the other ship.

Boats (ships with one deck) often handle collisions differently due to their smaller size and reduced mass. This is explained fully in the upcoming Boats section *(p. 92)*.

◊ **SHIP TO STATIONARY OBJECT**

If a ship sails bow-first or stern-first at speed into a large stationary object or terrain piece like dock or an exposed rock, damage is done to the hull of the ship.

If this occurs, the hull takes damage equal to the number of decks of the colliding ship. The ship also Runs Aground.

If a ship hits an object as described above with its side (like glancing off of a rock while executing a forward Turn at speed), then the ship takes hull damage as described above. The controlling player must also roll one d10. On a 6+ the ship has Run Aground.

A ship that drifts into a terrain piece or hits terrain as it is moving "directly away" from another ship does not take any damage and does not Run Aground.

Units aboard a ship that has suffered a collision are unaffected.

◊ **SHIPS COLLIDING WITH UNITS**

If a situation arises where ship or boat collides with a unit (for example, if a unit in shallow water along a shoreline has a boat drift into it), simply move the unit out of the way or in the direction it would be pushed by the ship, whichever movement is less. Make sure the unit is still Cohesive at the end of the move. The unit is otherwise unaffected by the collision.

8.6 Throwing & Releasing Grapples

Throwing grapples is a versatile action that pulls a ship to another ship, a ship to a stationary object, or an object to a ship.

Grapples can be thrown to:

» Pull a ship into contact with another ship.

» Moor a ship to a dock (or a similar terrain feature).

» Retrieve objects in the water (possibly useful in some Scenarios).

A unit on a ship that is within 3" of another ship or appropriate object may spend an action to throw grapples to it.

The target number for the test 5+. If the attempt fails, nothing happens. If the attempt is successful, see the rules below.

If the grappled target is a ship:

» the smaller ship (the one with fewer decks) is moved directly toward the deck holding the unit that threw the grapples onto the larger ship until the two ships touch.

» If both ships are the same size (have the same number of decks), the ship that threw grapples moves toward the target ship until the two ships closest decks touch.

» If the movement described above is not possible for some reason, (for example, one of the ships is Anchored), move the other ship into contact instead.

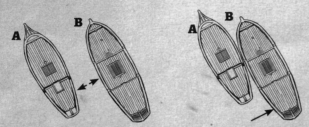

Figure 60: *Ship A (with 2 decks) throws grapples with a unit on its rearmost deck, to the middlemost deck of the 3 decked ship (ship B). The grapple is successful, and ship A is pulled to ship B so the two aforementioned decks touch.*

If the grappled target is an object:

» A ship of any size is moved directly toward a stationary object until the closest deck comes in contact with it.

» A floating or unrestrained smaller object is pulled to the deck of the ship that contains the unit that is throwing grapples.

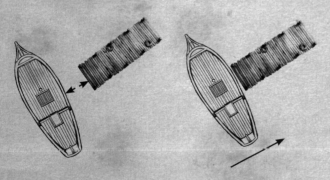

Figure 61: *A unit on the forward deck of a ship throws grapples to a dock. The attempt is successful, so the ship is pulled to the dock.*

MOVEMENT WHEN SHIPS ARE CONNECTED BY GRAPPLES

When two ships come into contact as a result of a successful grapple, it does not count as a collision, and the ships do not become fouled (*see Collisions p. 87*).

Ships that are grappled to a stationary object or terrain feature (like a dock) don't move until grapples are released.

Two (or more) ships that are grappled together may only drift when movement is taken, unless at least one is anchored.

All ships grappled together count as one ship for the purposes of drifting, and follow the normal rules described above in Ship Movement. Keep in mind that players may alternate moving the grappled ships depending on when units are activated (*see Figure 62*).

For example, two enemy ships start a turn grappled together. Following the normal rules for ship movement, the ships will move during the first activation, last activation, and during an activation in between, so long as they remain grappled together.

Therefore, the first player to activate a unit will drift the grappled ships, as well as the last player to activate a unit. Either player can drift the ships on an activation in between if it hasn't already been done by the other player.

Pick one of the grappled ships to determine which way all the attached ships drift. (It does not need to be the same ship every time it drifts).

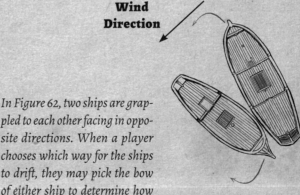

Wind Direction

In Figure 62, two ships are grappled to each other facing in opposite directions. When a player chooses which way for the ships to drift, they may pick the bow of either ship to determine how they turn away from the wind.

Figure 62

Boats (ships with one deck) handle movement when grappled differently due to their smaller size and reduced mass. This is explained fully in the Boats section (*p. 92*).

The rules for drifting described above can also be used in a situation when there is a ship with no crew controlling it (like an abandoned boat or drifting ship objective in a scenario).

RELEASING GRAPPLES

A successfully grappled ship or object is considered grappled until:

> » A unit on the ship that threw the grapples spends an action to release them.

> » An enemy unit spends an action cuts grapples. *(See Boarding Actions below.)*

Grapples may be released only if there are no enemy units on any ships that are connected by grapples.

No matter how grapples are released, the ship with the unit that released grapples may immediately move up to 3" directly away from the ship or terrain feature it was previously attached to. If this movement isn't possible, the other ship moves instead. *(See Collisions above)*.

If a ship is destroyed while grappled, the grapples release immediately and the destroyed ship (and all its crew) is removed from the game as normal.

8.7 *Ship Combat*

Combat with ships follows all standard rules for movement, access, and combat as outlined in the Structures section, unless they are modified by the rules below.

8.8 *Ships &* *Melee Combat*

BOARDING ACTIONS

To initiate a Melee Combat between two ships, the ships must be touching, either by being fouled or successfully grappled.

Once the ships are touching, a unit may Charge from their deck to engage enemy units in any of the opposing ship's decks as long as they are within 1" of each other. All standard rules for resolving Melee Combat within Structures apply.

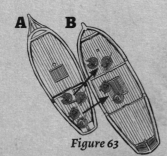

Figure 63

In Figure 63, a unit on the rearmost deck of Ship A may Charge units on the forward or middle decks of Ship B because they are within 1" of each other, but not the rearmost deck because it is more than 1" away.

If all Melee Combat has ended, and there are no enemy models aboard any ships, the ship's controlling player may immediately take an action with a unit to cut grapples. *(See Releasing Grapples above.)*

If during a boarding action all enemy models from a ship are removed as Casualties, the ship is captured. The capturing unit (and the player controlling it) are now in control of that ship.

8.9 *Ships &* *Ranged Combat*

TARGETING SHIPS

When targeting a ship with a Ranged Attack, you may choose to aim at the Hull or the Rigging.

◊ FIRING ON THE HULL

Like other Structures, only Artillery (except Swivels) can target and damage the deck of a ship. Units on a deck may be targeted with Small Arms (and Swivels) as usual.

When firing on a Hull deck (or the units on a deck), pick a specific deck to target, and remember to measure the closest points between the attacker and the deck to determine the range penalty.

Units in a deck section that is struck by Cannons will take one hit for each hit on that section, as is typical with Structures. The reinforced timber construction of a ship Hull provides all models on a deck with Hard Cover.

◊ FIRING ON THE RIGGING

Rigging may not be targeted with Cannons if the target ship is within 10". Small Arms and Swivels may still target the Rigging within 10".

When firing at the Rigging, use the corresponding Hull decks to measure to and determine the range penalty, not the actual masts and rigging of the ship being targeted.

If there are units in the Rigging (because of the Fighting Top ship trait), that unit will take hits when the Rigging takes damage from Artillery, just like any other Structure. Units in the Rigging to not count as being in Hard Cover.

When the Rigging takes any damage, there is also a chance that debris will fall and harm models on the deck below. To reflect this, every 2 points of damage inflicted on the ship's Rigging (rounded down) will cause one hit on units within the deck section where the Rigging is located. Ranged Saves may be taken as normal.

◊ SMALL ARMS VS. RIGGING

Units with Small Arms and Swivels may attempt to damage a ship's Rigging with a Ranged Attack. These less powerful weapons cannot do massive damage like cannon fire can. Instead, units with Small Arms can try to compromise the Rigging by shooting out the smaller, delicate sail components, like lines or blocks.

To represent the difficulty and reduced effectiveness of this, a unit firing on the Rigging with Small Arms and Swivels must roll 2 successful hits to score one hit on the Rigging.

Small Arms and Swivels can score a Lucky Hit on the Rigging, but the attacking unit must roll at least two natural 10s on the Shoot Test to do so. Small Arms and Swivels may never score any Critical Hits on Rigging.

If there are units in the Rigging (because of the Fighting Top ship trait), that unit will NOT take hits when the Rigging takes damage from Small Arms. (it must be targeted separately).

ARTILLERY ON SHIPS

A ship's Artillery are always assigned to a particular deck of the ship. Cannons may be placed in a section of the ship's hull that has gun ports (or swivel mounts in the case of Swivels).

The maximum number of Cannon and Swivels that a ship can carry (and how they are distributed per deck) is listed on its ship card. Buying Artillery for Ships is explained further in the Creating a Force section (p. 94).

Artillery cannot be removed from the ship or moved between decks during the course of battle. As mentioned in earlier in the rules, all Artillery aboard the ship must be assigned to units before the start of the battle

Unlike Artillery on field carriages or guns in a battery, a ship's Arc of Fire for a Cannon is the width of the deck from which it is fired. When determining Arc of Fire, use the part of the deck that can hold models to draw your arc from, not decorative parts such as the head rails and bowsprit (*see Figure 64*). Due to their smaller size and greater flexibility, Swivels have a 360° Arc of Fire.

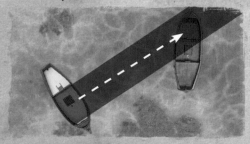

Figure 64: *The gun deck (front deck) of the sloop can target the middle or front deck of the enemy brigantine.*

RAKING SHOTS

A Raking Shot occurs when a ship is fired upon along its length by Cannons, which can cause great damage to ship and crew alike. Raking Shots are especially devastating when fired into the stern of an enemy ship.

To attempt a Raking Shot, the attacking ship's Artillery must be able to draw a straight line from the section from which it is firing, along the defending ship's center line, which exits out the opposite end.

Raking Shots can only be taken along the Hull of an enemy ship. They have no extra effect on the Rigging.

When a Raking Shot enters through the bow, every successful hit counts as two hits.

When a Raking Shot enters though the stern, the Fortitude of the ship counts as one less than its current value (to a minimum of 1) for that attack only, and every successful hit counts as two hits.

Casualties must be taken from all decks of the ship, working backward from the deck that was hit first. Distribute hits as evenly as possible.

For example, a 3 decked ship has 2 units on each deck, and takes 4 hits from a Raking Shot that enters through the bow. Both units on the foredeck take one hit each, both units on the middle deck takes one hit each, and the units on the rearmost deck do not take any hits.

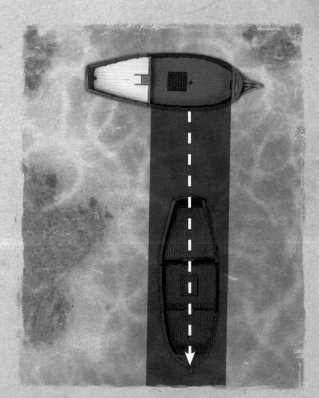

Figure 65: *A Raking Shot through the stern.*

8.10 *Boats*

Ships with one deck are considered boats. Boats are smaller, lightly constructed vessels mainly used for moving units from ship to shore or to another vessel. Boats are usually (but not always) included in a force as an addition when purchasing a larger ship.

Boats follow all the rules for ships as explained above, with the following additions and exceptions:

TARGETING BOATS

Boats may have Sails and Rigging like larger ships, but the Rigging on boats is much smaller and may not be targeted separately. The only location that may be targeted on a boat is the Hull.

LIGHT RIGGING

Due to the light construction of a boat's sails, there is no negative effect to the Rigging of a boat that exceeds its Top Speed or fails an Advanced Maneuver.

THROWING GRAPPLES FROM BOATS

Boats resolve throwing grapples exactly like larger ships, but the results are sometimes different due to a boat's smaller size.

If the grappled target is a ship:

» the boat is moved directly toward the target deck of a larger ship until the two ships touch.

» If both ships are boats, the boat that threw grapples moves toward the target boat until the two touch.

If the grappled target is an object:

» A boat is moved directly toward a stationary object until the boat comes in contact with it.

» A floating or unrestrained smaller object is pulled into the boat.

MOVEMENT WHEN BOATS ARE CONNECTED BY GRAPPLES

Boats have no effect on the speed and movement of larger ships (those with 2 or more decks). Therefore, a boat that is grappled to a larger ship does not cause either to drift, not even if the boat is anchored.

If a boat is grappled to another boat, however, they will drift exactly as described above in Movement When Ships Are Connected by Grapples.

COLLISIONS IN BOATS

◊ BOAT TO SHIP

When a boat collides with a ship, nothing happens to the ship or the boat, and neither can become fouled as a result.

When a ship collides with a boat, that's very bad for the boat:

» A boat struck by a ship takes twice the amount of damage as a ship-to-ship collision (*see Collisions p. 87*) as damage to the boats Hull, and the boat is pushed directly away 3". The ship is unaffected.

» Units on a boat that is struck must roll Saves to avoid taking Casualties as usual, but the Save is a flat 7+ to avoid being thrown overboard.

◊ BOAT TO BOAT

When a boat collides with another boat, it is resolved exactly like a larger ship to ship collision as described earlier in the rules.

Boats take damage when running into stationary objects in the same way the larger ships do.

TOWING BOATS

Boats that are purchased as an addition to a ship can be towed behind it unmanned until they are needed. To represent this, place all unmanned boats within 1" of the stern of the ship they are connected to at the end of the ship's movement. Towed boats remain behind the stern until they are used (*see below*).

◊ LAUNCHING BOATS FROM SHIPS

A unit on board a ship can spend an action to pull a towed boat up alongside the deck that unit occupies. Any unit in that deck section may then take Move actions to move onto the boat, but only if the ship is moving at 3" or slower.

When either a unit on the deck section or in the boat releases the grapples, the boat moves 3" directly away from the ship, and is considered to be launched.

A boat that has launched starts with its sail setting at 0", so actions must be taken to either increase the Sail Setting or man the Sweeps, otherwise the boat will drift when moved.

An unoccupied boat (either drifting within 3" or grappled alongside a ship) may be moved back into a towed position if a unit on the ship takes an action to do so.

9
Creating a Force

9.1 *How to Build a Force*

All players must first agree on a points limit. Once a point limit is agreed upon, each player then chooses a commander and an affiliated faction they would like to play. Each player then uses the points to "buy" units, ships, and potential fortifications available to that faction to build their force.

1. DETERMINE POINTS LIMIT

Each game must have a set points limit agreed upon by all the players. This is the total pool of points that each player uses to construct a force.

The game plays best with forces of between 100 and 400 points per player.

> » 100 points is ideal for beginners or players looking for a quick game of around an hour.

> » 200 points provides for a good game, averaging around 2 hours.

> » 400 points will produce a big game that can last an evening.

We suggest that a player does not build a single force that is greater than 400 pts.

The more points allowed for building a force, the larger it will be. Be ready to supply enough models when playing a big game.

2. SELECT A COMMANDER & A FACTION

The descriptions of the commanders in the next section describe each commander's point cost, stats, and special skills, as well as the factions that they may lead. Each player pays the listed point cost to pick a commander to lead their force.

Players may pick the same Standard commander, but may not take the same Legendary commander unless all players agree to allow it.

After a commander is chosen and paid for, the player picks an eligible faction that commander may lead, and buys units for their force (see below).

3. DETERMINE UNIT SIZE

The minimum and maximum number of models that can be included in a unit is dependent on the points limit of the force you are building.

The base unit size for a game of a 100 points or less is 3 to 8 models. Add +1 to the minimum unit size and +4 to the maximum unit size for each 100 points of the points limit.

For example, for a 350-point game, the standard unit size for all forces would be 6 to 20 models.

4. SELECT UNITS

When selecting units, the listed point cost is paid for each model in the unit. (The point cost for models is listed on their unit card, or in the Factions section of the rules).

A unit must have the minimum and maximum model count as noted above in Determine Unit Size. Each unit must consist of the same model type, but not necessarily the same types of weapons.

A faction list will always have 2 sections: Core units and Support units

Core Units represent troops that are the basis of that faction's fighting force. A force may include any of the units listed in this section, and any number of those units may be fielded. A force's commander must begin the game attached to a Core unit.

Support Units usually belong to the same nationality but are not typically part of a faction's organizational structure.

For every 2 Core units included in a force, a single Support unit may be included in that force as well.

For example, a force with 4 Core units could also field up to 2 Support units.

When purchasing models for units:

» If an Experience Level upgrade (or downgrade) is given to a unit, all units of that same type must take it as well.

For example, if a unit is upgraded from Inexperienced to Trained, all units of the same type in the force must also be upgraded to Trained.

» The above does not apply if units have different weapon or equipment options.

For example, if two units of Sea Dogs both have the option to field a Blunderbuss, one unit can take one but the other unit does not have to.

5. SELECT SCENARIO

This is a good time to select which scenario will be played, either by randomly rolling one or by choosing one mutually agreeable to both players (see Scenarios). With a scenario chosen at this point (and attacker/defender determined), both players can better pick the appropriate ships or fortifications when building their force.

6. SELECT SHIPS & FORTIFICATIONS

All current factions have the option to include ships and boats as part of their force. If a force includes ships, the battlefield must include suitable water terrain (See Scenarios for more details *p. 132*).

Simple fortifications may often be purchased by the defending force in a scenario, if appropriate. The list of fortifications, their point costs, and their rules are found in the Scenario Special Rules section.

7. OUTFIT SHIPS & FORTIFICATIONS

Ships do not include Artillery in their points value. Artillery must be purchased separately, and the type of Artillery that can be added to a ship depends on its Size:

» All ships (including boats) may carry Swivels.

» Size 2 and 3 ships may carry Light or Medium Cannons.

» Size 4 ships may carry Light, Medium, or Heavy Cannons.

Any ship may be outfitted with any number of Artillery pieces as long as the total number does not exceed its Cannon or Swivel limit. Guns must be placed on the decks within the limits indicated on the ship's card or the Ship Stat Summary table *(p. 121)*.

Cannons must be added to ships in pairs, and must be represented equally on both sides of the ship. The pairs of cannons may of be different types.

For example, a Sloop could field 2 pair of Light Cannon and one pair of Medium. Therefore, the Sloop would have one Medium and two Light Cannons facing both starboard and larboard.

Swivels may be added individually, and on any deck as indicated by the ship's card or the Ship Stat Summary table.

Each ship size 2 and above may also include a number of longboats equal to its number of decks (which must be purchased separately).

The Ship Stat Summary and Artillery Stats Chart are found after the Commander and Factions sections to aid players with purchasing and outfitting ships (p. 121).

9.2 Commanders

Force commanders are listed below by nationality. The factions that a commander may lead are also listed in their descriptions, and are detailed in the next section. Detailed descriptions of the Special Rules are found immediately after the Factions section.

SPANISH COMMANDERS

STANDARD
SPANISH MILITIA COMMANDERS
May lead any Spanish Caribbean Militia force.

UNTESTED: 0 POINTS

MAIN WEAPONS:	Pistol, Standard Melee Weapon
SIDE ARMS:	None
COMMAND RANGE:	8"
COMMAND POINTS:	1
SPECIAL RULES:	Ruthless

EXPERIENCED: 15 POINTS

MAIN WEAPONS:	Pistol, Standard Melee Weapon
SIDE ARMS:	None
COMMAND RANGE:	12"
COMMAND POINTS:	2
SPECIAL RULES:	Ruthless and Inspiring

SEASONED: 25 POINTS

MAIN WEAPONS:	Pistol, Standard Melee Weapon
SIDE ARMS:	None
COMMAND RANGE:	16"
COMMAND POINTS:	2
SPECIAL RULES:	Ruthless, Inspiring, High-Standing and Well-Equipped

STANDARD
GUARDA COSTA COMMANDERS
May lead any Guarda Costa force.

UNTESTED: 0 POINTS

MAIN WEAPONS:	Pistol, Standard Melee Weapon
SIDE ARMS:	None
COMMAND RANGE:	4"
COMMAND POINTS:	1
SPECIAL RULES:	Ruthless

EXPERIENCED: 15 POINTS

MAIN WEAPONS:	Pistol, Standard Melee Weapon
SIDE ARMS:	None
COMMAND RANGE:	8"
COMMAND POINTS:	2
SPECIAL RULES:	Ruthless, Broadside, and Inspiring

SEASONED: 25 POINTS

MAIN WEAPONS:	Pistol, Standard Melee Weapon
SIDE ARMS:	None
COMMAND RANGE:	12"
COMMAND POINTS:	2
SPECIAL RULES:	Ruthless, Broadside, Inspiring, and Commodore

HISTORIC SPANISH COMMANDERS

◊ DON FRANCISCO

The experiment at peace in the Spanish Main was short lived. By as early as April 1669 Spanish governors in the Caribbean had begun reissuing commissions against the English and, following a brief attempt at salvaging peace in the wake of Morgan's Panama expedition, all efforts were abandoned at the outbreak of the Franco-Spanish War in 1673. Of the corsairs active throughout this period, Captain Don Francisco was among the longest tenured and most accomplished. He was one of the chief agitators during the supposed times of peace in the late 1660s and early 1670s, infamously claiming the Amity of Bristol, which was well laden with goods. In 1673 he resumed his sea roving, taking English and French prizes with impunity, probably well beyond his legal right. On one occasion, the commander of a ship which Captain Don Francisco had recently captured, looted, and scuttled, demanded to see Francisco's commission, to which he replied "my flag is my commission" before releasing his captives by longboat into the sea.

25 POINTS
May lead any Guarda Costa force.

MAIN WEAPONS:	Pistol, Standard Melee Weapon
SIDE ARMS:	None
COMMAND RANGE:	12"
COMMAND POINTS:	2
SPECIAL RULES:	Determination, Commodore, Broadside, and Tough

» **Determination:** All Trained and Veteran units in this force must exchange the Ruthless Special Rule for Tough.

◊ MATEO ALONSO DE HUIDOBRO

The garrison commander of Veracruz, Mateo Alonso de Huidobro, was a capable tactician both on land and at sea. Being known for his naval competence, the Mexican viceroy often charged him and his militia to apprehend local interlopers. One such occasion was on August 14, 1673, where he displayed his versatility at Laguna de Términos. Being made aware of two pirate vessels which had taken refuge in the lagoon, de Huidobro assaulted their on shore camp, quickly routed the rouges to their ships and proceeded to make chase. The smaller brigantines initially eluded his Frigate through the costal shoals, but were eventually intercepted and easily overcome by de Huidobro's militia.

30 POINTS
May lead any Spanish Caribbean Militia force

MAIN WEAPONS:	Pistol, Standard Melee Weapon
SIDE ARMS:	None
COMMAND RANGE:	12"
COMMAND POINTS:	3
SPECIAL RULES:	Ruthless, Sailors, Broadside and, Commodore

◊ PHILIP FITZGERALD

Captain Phillip Fitzgerald was an Irish Catholic who captured the religious and national tensions of the period perhaps as well as any one man could. After his crew fell victim to a betrayal by the English crown, he defected to his catholic cousins in Havana, taking a Guarda Costa commission in 1672. His ambitions in the Caribbean are best expressed by the testimony of Matthew Fox, which was related thus in an official statement: "Captain Fitzgerald, an Irish Papist ... used him and his countrymen barbarously, giving no reason but that his countrymen were ill-used by the English 24 years ago, and he should never be satisfied with English blood, but could drink it as freely as water when he was adry." His purpose was to exact retribution through terror, using a variety of tactics to reach this end. On one occasion, before El Morro castle in Havana, he converted his masts into gallows and displayed his victims to the English captors who were laboring in the fortification. By 1674, he had incensed the English so greatly that even Spain agreed his crusade should be brought to an end. The Queen stripped his commission and ordered his arrest, though there is no evidence that he was ever apprehended.

20 POINTS
May lead any Guarda Costa force.

MAIN WEAPONS:	Pistol, Standard Melee Weapon
SIDE ARMS:	None
COMMAND RANGE:	8"
COMMAND POINTS:	2
SPECIAL RULES:	Ruthless, Vendetta: English, Broadside, Commodore, and Inspiring

» **Vendetta: English:** When fighting against any English force, this force may re-roll one failed die in any Rally test.

◊ CRISTOBAL ARNALDO DE ISSASI

Cristobal Arnaldo de Isassi spent years mastering the art of guerilla fighting while resisting English occupation in Jamaica. Having gained a reputation for his unique skill set, he was once again called upon to lead an inferior contingent of Spanish Militiamen against the invasion force of Commodore Myngs at Santiago de Cuba in 1662.

25 POINTS
May lead any Spanish Caribbean Militia force

MAIN WEAPONS:	Pistol, Standard Melee Weapon
SIDE ARMS:	None
COMMAND RANGE:	12"
COMMAND POINTS:	2
SPECIAL RULES:	Ruthless, Guerrilla Commander, Elusive, and Scouts

» **Guerrilla Commander:** Friendly units within the Command Range of this commander gain the Skirmishers Special Rule.

LEGENDARY SPANISH COMMANDER

◊ MANUEL RIVERO DE PARDAL

While it is difficult to call him a romantic, as he was not far enough removed from the Middle Ages to refer to his notions of chivalry as sentimental, Manuel Rivero de Pardal was certainly cut from that sort of cloth. There is no question that he sought personal glory, as did most every sea rover of his time, but unlike those other sea rovers, Pardal was also moved by a notion that his quest was nobel, and his cause pure. Pardal seemed to be passionately and genuinely motivated by an ideal: that the English were encroaching on divinely appointed territory. For him, the Anglo conquest of Jamaica was an intolerable heresy, and his indignation on this matter would prove to be a source of inspiration for the Spanish inhabitants of the new world. When no other Spanish captain would take a commission against the English, Rivero de Pardal managed to fill his 14 gun light frigate, San Pedro y La Fama, with 70 to 80 willing volunteers. His success would eventually inspire other captains as well, and culminate in a resurgence of Spanish privateers on the Spanish Main.

As passionate as he was, it may just as easily be said that it was megalomania that caused him to believe he was worthy of such lofty ambitions. He was known as a braggart,

being called the "vaporing captain" by his English rivals, and it is likely that his conceit was not exaggerated. He often spoke of such exploits as burning a fishing village to the ground as though they were major military victories, worthy of the annals of history. Between scouring the waves for victims and celebrating his triumphs at ports, he even found time to write an epic poem in his own honor, claiming in it that "the [people] all tremble . . . at my name." The most notable instance of his vainglory is undoubtedly the famous challenge he nailed to a tree on the Jamaican coasts, in which he wrote, "I come to seek General Morgan . . . I crave he would come out upon the coast and seek me, that he might see the valour of the Spaniards." This incensed the Jamaicans to no end, and they were quick to counter his egoism with disparagements. In one such account, a certain Edward Stanton, in reporting his eagerness to meet Rivero de Pardal at sea, states, "[it is said] he is afraid of the very shadow of a ship." The historical record, as a result, sometimes reveals Rivero de Pardal to be a sort of "Don Quixote" character, but in truth he appeared to exhibit the prudence and composure of a very capable commander.

Evidence of his competence can be cited in the account of his bout with Captain Bart. It was Feburary 1670 and Rivero de Pardal was returning from his first expedition when he learned that the renowned buccaneer was in Spanish waters. Upon locating Spiedrike's vessel, he hoisted English colors and drew near to hail, positioning himself carefully so that the smaller sloop would have no avenue of escape. Then, when Rivero de Pardal perceived the moment was right, he bellowed across the waves, "Defend yourself, dog, I come as punishment for heretics!" which he followed with a broadside. The ensuing battle is often cited to sing the praises of Bart's glorious last stand, in which his crew of 18 killed or wounded 36 from Rivero de Pardal's brimming vessel. What is perhaps even more impressive, however, is that Pardal managed to maintain the morale of his inexperienced crew while suffering such devastating losses and go on to win the day. This kind of resolve was uncommon among the inhabitants of the New World, and the following account of his engagement with John Morris of the Dolphin suggests that Pardal's leadership was the variable that had brought them victory.

In October of the same year, a storm forced Pardal's San Pedro y La Fama into a bay at the east end of Cuba, where he happened upon the Dolphin and its 60 men, who likewise were seeking refuge. Being delighted at this opportunity, Pardal made preparations for an early morning engagement, as the sun has already begun to set. It was Morris, however, who took the initiative and engaged La Fama before first light struck, boarding her on the first attempt. Seeing that his stunned crew began to waver, Pardal stepped to the fore in an effort to preserve the vigor of his men. Unfortunately, death found him that day, receiving as a reward for his gallantry a musket ball to the neck. With the source of their valor being vanquished, Pardal's men did not find the same courage that earned them victory against Bart. The Spaniards all scrambled overboard, leaving San Pedro y La Fama as an English prize.

32 POINTS

May lead any Spanish Caribbean Militia, Guarda Costa, or Los Cosarios de Pardal force.

MAIN WEAPONS:	Brace of Pistols, Standard Melee Weapon
SIDE ARMS:	None
COMMAND RANGE:	20"
COMMAND POINTS:	3
SPECIAL RULES:	Very Inspiring, Broadside, High Standing, Ruthless, Sailors, and Well-Equipped

ENGLISH COMMANDERS

STANDARD
ENGLISH MILITIA COMMANDERS
May lead any English Caribbean Militia force.

UNTESTED: 0 POINTS

MAIN WEAPONS:	Pistol, Standard Melee Weapon
SIDE ARMS:	None
COMMAND RANGE:	8"
COMMAND POINTS:	1
SPECIAL RULES:	None

EXPERIENCED: 15 POINTS

MAIN WEAPONS:	Pistol, Standard Melee Weapon
SIDE ARMS:	None
COMMAND RANGE:	12"
COMMAND POINTS:	2
SPECIAL RULES:	Inspiring

SEASONED: 25 POINTS

MAIN WEAPONS:	Pistol, Standard Melee Weapon
SIDE ARMS:	None
COMMAND RANGE:	16"
COMMAND POINTS:	2
SPECIAL RULES:	Inspiring, Expertly Drilled, and High Standing

STANDARD
ENGLISH BUCCANEER COMMANDERS
May lead any English Buccaneer or
Brethren of the Coast force.

UNTESTED: 0 POINTS

MAIN WEAPONS:	Brace of Pistols, Standard Melee Weapon
SIDE ARMS:	None
COMMAND RANGE:	4"
COMMAND POINTS:	1
SPECIAL RULES:	None

EXPERIENCED: 15 POINTS

MAIN WEAPONS:	Brace of Pistols, Standard Melee Weapon
SIDE ARMS:	None
COMMAND RANGE:	8"
COMMAND POINTS:	2
SPECIAL RULES:	Lead by Example

SEASONED: 25 POINTS

MAIN WEAPONS:	Brace of Pistols, Standard Melee Weapon
SIDE ARMS:	None
COMMAND RANGE:	16"
COMMAND POINTS:	2
SPECIAL RULES:	Lead by Example, Commodore, and Broadside

HISTORIC ENGLISH COMMANDERS

◊ COLONEL EDWARD MORGAN

Lieutenant Governor of Jamaica and uncle of Sir Henry Morgan, Colonel Edward Morgan was an energetic leader who possessed an imposing character by which he commanded loyalty and obedience from his men. He was a battle-hardened veteran of the Thirty Years War and the English Civil War who was known to urge his forces to victory through sheer force of will. In light of the impending Anglo-Dutch conflict, he was charged by Governor Modyford in February 1665 to seize Dutch possessions in the Caribbean. In the first conflict of the expedition, Morgan achieved a swift victory over the garrison of Saint Eustatius with a ferocious assault, but had himself succumbed to exhaustion and died during the invasion.

25 POINTS
May lead any English Caribbean Militia force.

MAIN WEAPONS:	Pistol, Standard Melee Weapon
SIDE ARMS:	None
COMMAND RANGE:	12"
COMMAND POINTS:	2
SPECIAL RULES:	Motivated, Heat Stroke, Inspiring, and Expertly Drilled

» **Motivated:** When this commander uses a Command Point to give a unit an action, this commander's unit may take a point of Fatigue to give it an additional action.

» **Heat Stroke:** If this model's unit become Shaken, roll a d10. If the result is 6+, this commander is removed as a Casualty.

◊ SIR THOMAS WHETSTONE

Sir Thomas Whetstone was the Royalist nephew of Oliver Cromwell, whose allegiance had shifted recently with the changing political tide. His family ties to the former Lord Protector made him an unwelcomed presence in the king's court and he was eventually forced to start a new life in Jamaica. He proved to be incredibly resourceful. Before long he acquired a vessel, which was mostly crewed by Natives, and engaged in the lucrative business of robbing the Spanish. In October 1662 he was discovered by Christopher Myngs, who saw the value in Whetstone's knowledge of the region, and employed his service as a captain on his expedition. By 1663, it seems that Whetstone had found his place in the new world, his ship being listed as one of the "private ships of war belonging to Jamaica."

30 POINTS
May lead any English Caribbean Militia force.

MAIN WEAPONS:	Brace of Pistols and Standard Melee Weapon
SIDE ARMS:	None
COMMAND RANGE:	12"
COMMAND POINTS:	3
SPECIAL RULES:	Unorthodox Force, Broadside, Sailors, and Inspiring

» **Unorthodox Force:** A force led by this commander may take Sea Dogs and Milicianos Indios as Core units.

◊ ROBERT SEARLE

Robert Searle was a well-known Buccaneer and trouble-maker who was spared from his rash and defiant character by his tactical brilliance. He was twice arrested for continually claiming Spanish prizes after his letter of marquees had been recalled, but was released on each occasion when the need arose for his superior military capabilities. One of these arrests was in response to his famous sacking of Saint Augustine in May 1668. The illicit raid earned him the ire of Governor Modyford of Jamaica, but also won him fame for his shrewd tactics in capturing the city. He was released from his incarceration on this occasion to join Henry Morgan on his Panama expedition, where his imprudence would finally catch up with him. Being charged by Morgan to quarantine the port of Panama, he chose instead to enjoy the booze and women he had recently procured, allowing the 400-ton Santísima Trinidad to escape with the riches of the city.

25 POINTS
May lead any English Buccaneer force.

MAIN WEAPONS:	Brace of Pistols or Buccaneer Gun, Standard Melee Weapon
SIDE ARMS:	None or Pistol (only if armed with a Buccaneer Gun)
COMMAND RANGE:	12"
COMMAND POINTS:	2
SPECIAL RULES:	Lead by Example, Aggressive Commander, Brawlers, and Broadside

» **Aggressive Commander:** All friendly units within this commander's Command Range gain the Hard Chargers Special Rule.

◊ BARNARD SPEIDRYKE

Affectionately known in Jamaica as "Captain Bart," Barnard Speidryke was a renowned Dutch buccaneer who sailed under the English Flag. He was killed in a fateful confrontation with Manuel Rivero de Pardal, but not before his humble crew of 18 slew 36 of Pardal's men. The outrage at his death was the catalyst of a chain of events which would eventually lead to Morgan's Panama Expedition.

25 POINTS
May lead any English Buccaneer force.

MAIN WEAPONS:	Brace of Pistols or Buccaneer Gun, Standard Melee Weapon
SIDE ARMS:	None or Pistol (only if armed with a Buccaneer gun)
COMMAND RANGE:	12"
COMMAND POINTS:	2
SPECIAL RULES:	Lead by Example, Very Inspiring, and Expert Broadside

» **Expert Broadside:** All Artillery fired during this commander's activation may be fired simultaneously. Additionally, if a 1 is rolled for any Critical Hit or Lucky Hit that is scored during a Broadside, it may be re-rolled.

LEGENDARY ENGLISH COMMANDER

◊ HENRY MORGAN

Henry Morgan was born to a Welsh family in the Old World, and had he remained there it is likely that his life would have been quite unremarkable. British society was a fixed structure with nearly impenetrable barriers, but the New World can be likened unto a primeval chaos, where a clever man with unbound ambitions could make for himself whatever life he chose. Henry Morgan was such a man. From obscurity he emerged as the most notorious commander in the Caribbean, whose name was undoubtedly uttered with curses and praises in the courts of kings. As the admiral of the Brethren of the Coasts, he regularly frustrated Spanish defenses against impossible odds, plundering the wealth of New Spain as freely as the wind carried his vessels. Some Spaniards called him El Drake, believing him to be the reincarnation of that dreaded pirate who, not too long before, ravaged the coasts of the Spanish Main. Morgan would in fact exceed Sir Francis Drake in many ways, becoming the greatest threat to Spanish hegemony in the new world.

From the outset, it is clear that Morgan saw the way of war as his avenue to opportunity. He likely entered the forge of Caribbean life as a low-ranking officer in the Cromwell expedition. By the time he appears on the historical record, he had achieved his first command as a captain in Admiral Christopher Myngs' Santiago expedition. Morgan learned much under the expert leadership of Myngs, and by 1668 he had accrued the wealth, fame, and experience to organize expeditions of his own. From here on, Morgan's career would be characterized by the same irrational boldness and razor-sharp intellect which was possessed by Alexander, Napoleon, and the other great conquerors of history.

His first major achievement, the sack of Portobello, captures perfectly the audaciousness of his vision. The siege itself was mostly ordinary in its execution; the most cunning — and controversial — innovation would have been the decision to approach El Castillo de Santiago behind a line of civilians and clergy. The boldness of the raid was the target itself. Portobello was a jewel in the crown of the Spanish Caribbean and a symbol of Spain's dominance in the region. The city was thought to host a Garrison of 350 men who populated 3 impressive fortresses of over 40 total guns. Additionally, an army of 800 from Panama could be mustered and set before the gates of the city within a week's time, placing a very narrow timetable for a successful siege. No corsair dared to challenge it. That is, until July 11, 1668. A sea raid was impossible due to the strength of the strongholds so, under the cover of night, Morgan approached in canoes with about 500 Buccaneers. Though the fortifications were, in truth, undermanned, and the artillery in disrepair, the swiftness and precision with which he organized his offensive was truly impressive. By the end of the second day all three forts were flying the English standard, at the cost of only 18 men.

Morgan had a wit to match his pluck. The president of Panama, Agustin Bracamonte, would discover this in the course of the negotiations for Portobello's ransom. Bracamonte initially refused to even consider Morgan's proposal, as he was a "corsair" and therefore an "inferior person . . ." Morgan, ever anxious to achieve a noble station in life, was clearly offended. Nonetheless, keeping his composure, he responded as follows, "Although your letter does not deserve a reply, since you call me a corsair, nevertheless I write you these few lines to ask you to come quickly. We are waiting for you with great pleasure and we have powder and ball with which to receive you . . . And since I do not believe that you have sufficient men to fight with me tomorrow, I will order all the poor prisoners to be freed so that they may go to help you." This was a bluff, but it was well placed; a price of 100,000 pesos was agreed upon for the return of the city. Bracamonte, being perplexed at how such a great city was taken, asked Morgan for a sample of the weapons used, imagining that they must have been of exceptional quality. Morgan obliged the president, sending him an ordinary pistol with a message stating that there would be no need to send it back, as he would be in Panama the following year to claim it. His cunning translated to the battlefield as well. On April 26, 1669, Morgan found himself trapped in the bay of Maracaibo. Between him and the only exit to the sea was the Armada de Barlovento, and its flagship, Magdalena, laden with 40 guns. Refusing surrender, Morgan sailed out to meet the fleet at sunrise, using to his advantage the cover of the morning mist. Morgan's flagship sailed straight for the Magdalena, drawing heavy fire as she went. As soon as the vessels had locked with grapples, the Spaniards leaped onto Morgan's ship in a frenzy, shocked to find only some planks dressed like men and some sailors in a canoe rowing away furiously in the distance. Moments later the vessel exploded. In a most unpredictable move, Morgan converted his flagship into a fire ship, destroying in moments Spain's strongest active vessel in the new world. In the confusion, Morgan overwhelmed the rest of the fleet and made his escape.

Sir Henry Morgan's greatest achievement was his triumph over Panama, but on this occasion his ambitions had taken him too far. The outrage in Madrid spilled over into London, and Morgan, along with Jamaica's governor Thomas Modyford, were arrested and sent to England for trial. But by the time he arrived in London relations in Europe had deteriorated, as they often did, and Morgan was instead knighted and installed as the lieutenant governor of Jamaica, where he lived out the rest of his days.

42 POINTS

May lead any English Caribbean Militia, English Buccaneer, Brethren of the Coast, or Morgan's Buccaneers force.

MAIN WEAPONS:	Brace of Pistols, Standard Melee Weapon
SIDE ARMS:	None
COMMAND RANGE:	20"
COMMAND POINTS:	3
SPECIAL RULES:	Very Inspiring, Broadside, Misfortune at Sea, God's Blessing or the Devils' Luck, and Lucky

» **Misfortune at Sea** – A force that this model is commanding may not spend Fortune Points to re-roll failed checks to Run Aground, attempt Repairs, change Sail Settings, or perform Advanced Maneuvers.

FRENCH COMMANDERS

STANDARD
FRENCH BUCCANEER COMMANDERS

May lead any French Buccaneer.

UNTESTED: 0 POINTS

MAIN WEAPONS:	Brace of Pistols, Standard Melee Weapon
SIDE ARMS:	None
COMMAND RANGE:	4"
COMMAND POINTS:	1
SPECIAL RULES:	None

EXPERIENCED: 15 POINTS

MAIN WEAPONS:	Brace of Pistols, Standard Melee Weapon
SIDE ARMS:	None
COMMAND RANGE:	8"
COMMAND POINTS:	2
SPECIAL RULES:	Lead by Example

SEASONED: 25 POINTS

MAIN WEAPONS:	Brace of Pistols, Standard Melee Weapon
SIDE ARMS:	None
COMMAND RANGE:	16"
COMMAND POINTS:	2
SPECIAL RULES:	Lead by Example, Commodore, and Broadside

HISTORIC FRENCH COMMANDERS

◊ MONBARS THE EXTERMINATOR

Monbars the Exterminator was the personification, perhaps even the manifestation, of the fear and awe which was inspired by the pirates of the Spanish Main. He was known to be terrible in appearance and methods, being gripped by a fiery indignation toward the Iberians. As the story goes, Monbar was a gentleman turned rogue, whose hatred of the Spanish began while learning of their cruelties towards the Natives during his studies, and was complete when he witnessed his uncle's death at the hands of a Spanish fleet. Although he was infamous for his savagery in combat, his nobel roots never left him. He was said to have drawn French, English, and Caribs alike under his command with his gentlemanly manner. And, like the "good gentleman" he was, he never killed in cold blood, as many other buccaneers were known to do. As for the exploits of The Exterminator, they are too grand and numerous to list in this present account. The legend of Monbars is so fantastic, in fact, that some modern historians have suggested that he never existed at all. For all of his conquests, only Exquemelin claims to have seen him with his own eyes. It may be the case that the exploits of the many anonymous Brethren Captains marauding in the Caribbean were incarnate in a single figure whose awe matched the collective dread they inspired. Whatever the case may be, Exquemelin's accounts tells us that the stories were thought to be true. And for the Spaniard who had his anxious eyes set on the horizon, he was certainly very real.

25 POINTS
May lead any French Buccaneer
or Brethren of the Coast force

MAIN WEAPONS:	Brace of Pistols or Buccaneer Gun, Standard Melee Weapon
SIDE ARMS:	None or Pistol (only if armed with a Buccaneer gun)
COMMAND RANGE:	12"
COMMAND POINTS:	2
SPECIAL RULES:	Lead by Example, Ruthless, Vendetta: Spanish, Broadside, and Unorthodox Force.

» **Vendetta: Spanish:** When fighting against any Spanish force, this force may re-roll one failed die in any Rally test.

» **Unorthodox Force:** A force led by this commander may take Milicianos Indios as Core units.

◊ ALEXANDRE BRAS DE FER ("IRON ARM")

Captain Alexandre Bras de Fer was described as a handsome, vigorous commander; modest in victory, giving credit to his crew rather than himself. The charismatic commander generally favored sailing alone, preferring to put his trust in his men rather than the commander of a fleet. It is unlikely that he ever had trouble finding crew to fill his ship. Along with his winning personality, he possessed an uncanny knack for finding good fortune, even in the worst situations. On one such instance Iron Arm's ship, being caught in the midst of a lightning storm, had been set ablaze, leaving him and his crew shipwrecked on a nearby island. Stranded and desperate for supplies, his men ventured into the island where they happened upon a Spanish crew who had come ashore to make camp. Seizing the opportunity, they overcame the unsuspecting sailors and claimed their ship along with its cargo.

20 POINTS
May lead any French Buccaneer force.

MAIN WEAPONS:	Brace of Pistols or Buccaneer Gun, Standard Melee Weapon
SIDE ARMS:	None or Pistol (only if armed with a Buccaneer gun)
COMMAND RANGE:	8"
COMMAND POINTS:	2
SPECIAL RULES:	Lead by Example, Inspiring, Lucky, and Broadside.

LEGENDARY FRENCH COMMANDER

◊ JEAN DAVID NAU (A.K.A FRANCOIS L'OLONNAIS)

"The fame of his cruelties . . . made him so well known through the Indies, that the Spaniards in his time would choose rather to die or sink fighting, than surrender, knowing they should have no mercy at his hands." Thus was the reputation of Jean David Nau, more commonly know as François l'Olonnais, according to Exquemelin. This reputation of his is well earned, for, if the historical record can be trusted, he was almost certainly a sociopath. But as he exceeded all men in atrocities, he did so in intrepidness as well. He was an inspiring commander, always leading from the front and never showing fear in the face of death. As was such, he had one of the most accomplished careers of any buccaneer captain in the Seventeenth century. At the high of his fame, he was the most sought after captain in Tortuga. In his final voyage he filled his vessels with over 700 volunteers, for it was widely understood that, while in l'Olonnais company, one was "safe . . . to the greatest dangers," and riches would come easily.

Only in the New World was a story such as his possible. L'Olinnais was shipped to the Caribbean under indentured servitude. Upon fulfilling his tenure, he traveled to Hispaniola and spent some there living among the Boucaniers. For unknown reasons he left that life, opting instead for a life of piracy. l'Olonnais excelled at violence, and he soon distinguished himself as a man of great capabilities. He was granted his first vessel by the governor of Tortuga, prudently trusting l'Olonnais to earn him great wealth. He enjoyed success in these early days, quickly gaining for himself that fearsome reputation for which he is remembered.

Of resourcefulness, he had a steady supply, and his first great misfortune would give him occasion to show it. While at sea, l'Olonnais was overwhelmed by a storm which appear near the coast of Campeche and utterly destroyed his ship. Many of his crew survived, but upon reaching the shore they were massacred by Spanish militiamen who were awaiting their arrival. l'Olonnais was wounded in the attack and had little hope of surviving with the militia approaching to survey the dead. Thinking quickly, he mingled the blood from his wound with some sand and smeared it on his face, then laid motionless among the dead. With his face being unrecognizable, he was left laying in the sand. Once his wound had healed he ventured into Campeche. Disguised as a Spaniard, he roamed the town for days, recruiting slaves and whatever outcasts he could before making his escape in two stolen canoes. Reports and celebration of the dreaded l'Olonnais and his supposed death spread quickly, so it must have come as quite a shock when a letter was received in Havana that he was spotted near Del los Cayos preparing to raid the village. A vessel of 10 guns and 90 men was dispatched to capture the pirate. Where others might have seen trouble, l'Olonnais saw opportunity. The vessel arrived at Del los Cayos in the early morning and just as the sun began to rise, the men boarded the ship from their canoes and engaged the Spaniards in a heated battle. In the end, it was François's men who carried the day, and he now had a ship to continue his depredations.

What followed was the first account of his many atrocities. Some captains would have ransomed the prisoners, some may have killed them all quickly and sailed off, but l'Olonnais had them brought before him, one by one, and beheaded. The last of the Spaniards, after being promised quarter for information, was killed in kind when he was exhausted of all he knew. For l'Olonnais, however, this was moderate conduct. When prisoners were not forth coming with information on ambushes or terrain or hidden riches, we was known to hack men to pieces and pull out their tongues before their comrades. On one occasion, when not even these methods sufficed, he was said to have cut open a man's breast, rip out his still-beating heart and "bite and gnaw it with his teeth, like a ravenous wolf . . ."

He carried this same viciousness with him onto the battlefield and instilled it in the men who followed him. He was indeed a very capable leader, inspiring his men to over come impossible odds. During the late spring of 1667, he found himself before the fortified city of Gibraltar, where much of the regions wealth had been hidden. The stronghold was well supplied with artillery, and the garrison outnumbered the filibusters. l'Olonnais, determined to claim his prize, delivered the following speech before leading this foolhardy assault: "we have good courage; we must either defend ourselves like good soldiers, or lose our lives with all the riches we have got. Do as I shall do, who am your captain. At other times we have fought with fewer men than we have in our company at present, and yet we have overcome great numbers . . . the more they are, the more glory, and the more riches we shall gain." It wouldn't be l'Olonnais, of course, if he didn't add the caveat, "but know ye, withal, that the first man who should show any fear, or the least apprehension thereof, I will pistol him with my own hands." They took the fortress that day, and lost many of their number doing so, making the survivors all the richer.

FRANCOIS L'OLONNAIS - 37 POINTS

May lead any French Buccaneer
or Flibustier Nau force.

MAIN WEAPONS:	Brace of Pistols, Standard Melee Weapon
SIDE ARMS:	None
COMMAND RANGE:	16"
COMMAND POINTS:	3
SPECIAL RULES:	Very Inspiring, Broadside, Ruthless, God's Blessing or the Devil's Luck and Terror.

» **Terror** – At the beginning of a battle, all enemy units must take a Resolve Test on 1 d10. If the test is failed, that unit gains one point of Fatigue.

9.3 *Factions*

All the factions are listed below, sorted by nationality. Firelock Games will be releasing more factions (and models for them) in future supplements.

SPAIN

 pain! Land of romance and Inquisition! New Spain, New Granada, and Peru, along with the adjacent islands, make up Spain in the New World, what we today know collectively as the Spanish Main of fact and fiction, of romance and reality. It is a grand empire, more diverse and colorful than any of the other European nations in the Americas. In fact, most of European-settled America is controlled by Spain, giving the Iberian kingdom great wealth from the silver, gold, and goods found here. But the Spanish crown has squandered its American wealth, and the Spanish empire is in decline. It cannot afford to defend its New World colonies as well as it must. Ashore it relies on fortifications, Spanish regulars in the larger towns and some small outposts, and local militias often augmented by Native Americans. At sea it relies on a small fleet known as the *Armada de Barlovento*, but it cannot be everywhere at once. *Guardas costas* (privately commissioned coast guards) provide local sea patrols, and armadillas—locally armed vessels—are sent out on specific occasions, but both are often as piratical as the buccaneers they defend against. Spanish defenses are typically weak: only the great treasure fleets remain well protected.

◊ SPANISH CARIBBEAN MILITIA

Spanish militia augment Spanish regulars, and typically outnumber them. The militia are composed primarily of three sorts: infantry and cavalry milicianos modelled on Spanish regulars; *lanceros* made up of hunters and workers; and Native American auxiliaries. The infantry are armed primarily with mosquetes (heavy matchlock muskets used with a rest), arcabuses (light matchlock muskets used without a stand), and often with escopetas (flintlocks muskets) used for hunting. Many carry cup-hilted rapiers or broadswords as well. Conventional cavalry are armed with flintlock carbines, pistols, and cup-hilted broadswords. *Lanceros* are armed with lance and machete; mounted lanceros often use a "hocksing iron" (a lance with a crescent-shaped blade for hamstringing wild cattle) insead. Native Americans are armed with bow and arrow. Often the milicianos' greatest shortcoming is too few veterans and firearms. *Milicianos* of all types are ethnically diverse, although often commanded by Spanish *Peninsulares* and *Criollos*. *Milicianos* include blooded veterans, merchant amateurs, haughty hidalgos, and bold workers, slaves, and Native Americans. All have one thing in common: they are fiercely proud.

FORCE SPECIAL RULES

This force may deploy a single unit with the Elusive or Skirmishers Special Rule following the "Lay in Wait" rules in the Scenarios section (*p. 144*).

CORE UNITS

Milicianos, Lanceros

SUPPORT UNITS

Marineros, Milicianos Indios

FORCE OPTIONS

GUERILLAS: Every unit in this force with the Drilled Special Rule may exchange that rule for the Elusive Special Rule.

MEN OF OLD SPAIN: All of the Miliciano units in this force may be upgraded from Inexperienced to Trained for 1 point per model. Lanceros may be upgraded from Trained to Veteran for 1 point per model.

◊ GUARDA COSTAS

Guardas costas are Spanish privateers commissioned for local coastal defense against smugglers and pirates—but often enough, are considered as outright pirates by the English, French, and Dutch. *Guardas costas* seize the hulls and arrest the crews of any foreign vessel found with *frutas de las Indias*—anything that might have been produced on the Spanish Main—aboard. They are mixed lot of Spanish and Portuguese *Peninsulares*, Spanish *Criollos*, Levanters, Italians, Corsicans, Native Americans, Africans, and mixed races, and are known to be as brutal as any buccaneer or flibustier, and likewise their captains as swashbuckling as any buccaneer or flibustier

FORCE SPECIAL RULES

» All Trained and Veteran units in this force gain the Well Equipped special rule.

» All units in this force with the Drilled special rule have the Sailors special rule instead.

» This force adds +2 when determining the attacker in a scenario.

CORE UNITS

Marineros, Milicianos

SUPPORT UNITS

Lanceros, Milicianos Indios

FORCE OPTIONS

VIZCAYNOS: All of the *Marinero* units in this force may be upgraded to Veterans for 1 point per model. All of the *Miliciano* units in this force may be upgraded to Trained for 1 point per model.

◊ LOS CORSARIOS DE PARDAL

This is the personal force of Rivero de Pardal. This Character must be chosen as this force's commander.

FORCE SPECIAL RULES

» Once per game and during Pardal's units activation, Pardal may spend a Command Point to issue a challenge to one enemy unit. Pardal's unit receives a -1 bonus to any Resolve Tests triggered by the challenged unit for the rest of the game. If Pardal's unit destroys the enemy unit, the enemy force gains a Strike Point. If Pardal's unit is destroyed by the challenged unit, Pardal's force gains a Strike Point.

» This force adds +3 when determining the attacker in a scenario.

CORE UNITS

Milicianos

SUPPORT UNITS

Marineros

FORCE OPTIONS

INEXPERIENCED CREW: For the cost of -1 point per model, this faction may take *Marineros* as Core units, but all *Marineros* are Inexperienced instead of Trained.

MARINES: All units in this force with the Drilled Special Rule may exchange it for the Sailors Special Rule instead.

SPANISH UNITS

◇ MILICIANOS

◇ LANCEROS

3 POINTS

Spanish militiamen made up the bulk of Spain's colonial troops. Usually armed with arquebuses, these troops were often poorly trained and inexperienced.

EXPERIENCE LEVEL:	Inexperienced
MAIN WEAPONS:	Matchlock Muskets, Standard Melee Weapons
SIDE ARMS:	None
FIGHT:	6/6
SHOOT:	7/8
RESOLVE:	6
SPECIAL RULES:	Drilled, Ruthless, and Poorly Equipped

5 POINTS

These Spanish Lancers were elite fighters who adapted the use of European pole-arms to their dense Caribbean environment. Masters of ambushing and stealth, these guerilla units moved swiftly through any terrain and were notoriously skilled in melee.

EXPERIENCE LEVEL:	Trained
MAIN WEAPONS:	Lances
SIDE ARMS:	None
FIGHT:	5/7
SHOOT:	-/6
RESOLVE:	5
SPECIAL RULES:	Skirmisher, Ruthless, Elusive, and Scouts

SPANISH UNITS

◇ MILICIANOS INDIOS

◇ MARINEROS

5 POINTS

Christianized Natives often fought with the Spanish as auxiliaries. They were adept with bows and arrows and masters of jungle fighting.

EXPERIENCE LEVEL:	Trained
MAIN WEAPONS:	Bows, Standard Melee Weapons
SIDE ARMS:	None
FIGHT:	5/8
SHOOT:	6/6
RESOLVE:	6
SPECIAL RULES:	Quick, Skirmisher, Elusive, and Scouts

4 POINTS

Spanish Sailors were excellent seamen, and those from the Bay of Biscay were thought of as especially skilled and brave. Equipped with pistols, they were known to be deadly in brawl.

EXPERIENCE LEVEL:	Trained
MAIN WEAPONS:	Pistols, Standard Melee Weapons
SIDE ARMS:	None
FIGHT:	5/7
SHOOT:	7/7
RESOLVE:	5
SPECIAL RULES:	Ruthless, Artillery Crew, Poorly Equipped, and Sailors

ENGLAND

I n many ways England has revealed itself in the Caribbean to be what Spain has long called it: a nation of pirates! For years, England was limited to Barbados and its sugar, molasses, and rum, and a few other small colonies in the Antilles, but with the capture of Jamaica from Spain—of doubtful lawfulness, but what can Spain do?—England has unleashed its rovers on its hated Inquisitorial enemy. "No peace beyond the line" is the justification, along with pretenses of reprisals against Spanish piracies, which are often in reprisal for piracies by English buccaneers. But England is not only a nation of sea dogs: it is also a nation of merchant traders, and by and by the latter come to rule. As trade with Spain becomes paramount, the buccaneers are slowly suppressed, and begin marauding into the South Sea—the Pacific Ocean, that is—coasts of the Spanish Main. Many are opposed to the suppression of the buccaneers, for they are the bulwark of defense at sea against enemy attack.

◊ ENGLISH CARIBBEAN MILITIA

The English Caribbean militias are the backbone of English defense in the New World. They are modeled as much, or more, on the English army as they are on the English trainbands, for there are few English regulars to be found in the Americas, and then often only during wartime. The militia are generally well armed: the infantry primarily with flintlock muskets, especially after the late 1670s, the cavalry with carbines, pistols, and broadswords. Many of the militias have red uniforms, modeled after the English redcoats. Wealthy planters are often the officers, with local tradesmen, indentured servants, and other working men, including slaves at times, serving in the ranks. Some cavalry units, as in England, are composed of gentlemen. Most of the English militia take pride in their service. They muster regularly, and in time of war are often called to arms. In Jamaica, much of the militia ranks are formed of buccaneers—but these sea rovers are often away at sea.

FORCE SPECIAL RULES

This force may re-roll any of its failed Fatigue and Rally test results during the game's first turn.

CORE UNITS

English Militia, Freebooters

SUPPORT UNITS

Sea Dogs

FORCE OPTIONS

HISPANIOLA VETERANS: All of the English Militia units in this force may be upgraded from Inexperienced to Trained for 1 point per model.

◊ ENGLISH BUCCANEERS

So famous are the English buccaneers that they hardly need explanation! Composed primarily of men from the British Islands and English New World colonies, they may also include men of other nations in their ranks. They are a broad spectrum in origin: mariners, former Cromwellian soldiers, former indentured servants, small planters disenchanted with the soil, tradesmen looking for a purportedly easier way to earn a living, common and uncommon adventurers, fishermen, turtlers, logwood cutters, smugglers, and even some former slaves are among their ranks. They are loyal to England, but only to a point: forbid them their Spanish prey, and they are as likely to serve the French as they are to accept an amnesty from the English crown. They are commonly armed with a flintlock musket (often the *fusil boucanier*), a cartouche box with thirty cartridges, a pistol or two, and a cutlass. They are proud of their martial abilities at sea and ashore, and consider themselves "true buccaneers and soldiers"—and also as privateers so that they may pretend they are never pirates.

FORCE SPECIAL RULES

» Once per game, this force's controlling player may discard all the Activation Cards in their hand and replace them with the same number of new cards without spending a Fortune Point.

» This force always adds +2 to it's roll to determine attacker.

CORE UNITS

Freebooters, Forlorn Hope, Sea Dogs

SUPPORT UNITS

English Militia, Flibustiers, Boucaniers

FORCE OPTIONS

OLD HANDS: All of the Freebooters, Sea Dogs and/or Forlorn Hope in this force may be upgraded from Trained to Veteran for 1 point per model.

◊ MORGAN'S BUCCANEERS

This is the personal force of Henry Morgan. This Character must be chosen as this force's commander.

FORCE SPECIAL RULES

» Once per turn, this force's controller may replace a revealed Activation Card with another card from their hand. This card replaces the original and determines initiative and actions for that activation.

» Once per game, this force's controlling player may discard all the Activation Cards in their hand and replace them with the same number of new cards without spending a Fortune Point.

» This force always adds +3 to its roll to determine attacker.

CORE UNITS

Freebooters, English Militia, Forlorn Hope

SUPPORT UNITS

Sea Dogs, Flibustier, Boucaniers

FORCE OPTIONS

OLD HANDS: All of the Freebooters and/or Forlorn Hope in this force may be upgraded from Trained to Veteran for 1 point per model. English Militia may be upgraded to trained for 1 point per model.

PANAMA INVASION FORCE: All Freebooter and Forlorn Hope units in this force may exchange the Fast Reload Special Rule for the Drilled Special Rule.

ENGLISH UNITS

◇ ENGLISH MILITIA

◇ FREEBOOTERS

3 POINTS

English Militia were generally better equipped than their Spanish counterparts. Usually armed with muskets, these units were drilled in typical European tactics.

EXPERIENCE LEVEL:	Inexperienced
MAIN WEAPONS:	Firelock Muskets, Standard Melee Weapons
SIDE ARMS:	None
FIGHT:	6/7
SHOOT:	7/8
RESOLVE:	5
SPECIAL RULES:	Drilled

6 POINTS

Freebooters were English New Worlders from all walks of life who mastered the musketry tactics of the old French boucaniers. They were skilled in all manners of combat, possessing notable proficiency with their muskets.

EXPERIENCE LEVEL:	Trained
MAIN WEAPONS:	Buccaneer Guns, Standard Melee Weapons
SIDE ARMS:	Pistols
FIGHT:	6/6
SHOOT:	6/7
RESOLVE:	5
SPECIAL RULES:	Ball & Shot, Fast Reload, Sailors, and Marksmen

ENGLISH UNITS

◇ FORLORN HOPE   ◇ SEA DOGS

7 POINTS

Forlorn Hope were sent ahead of Buccaneer raiding parties to foil ambushes and secure crucial strategic positions. They were typically equipped with muskets, pistols, and grenadoes, and were known for their fierce tenacity.

EXPERIENCE LEVEL:	Trained
MAIN WEAPONS:	Buccaneer Guns, Brace of Pistols, Standard Melee Weapons
SIDE ARMS:	Explosives
FIGHT:	6/6
SHOOT:	6/7
RESOLVE:	4
SPECIAL RULES:	Ball & Shot, Fast Reload, and Vanguard

WEAPON OPTIONS: In a unit of Forlorn Hope, one model in every four is also armed a single type of Explosive (grenado, firepot, or stinkpot: controlling player's choice) as a Main Weapon for no additional cost. A unit which has multiple models with Explosives may select different types.

4 POINTS

English sailors were masters of seamanship. Life at sea made them rugged and surly men who were hard to match in a melee.

EXPERIENCE LEVEL:	Trained
MAIN WEAPONS:	Pistols, Standard Melee Weapons
SIDE ARMS:	None
FIGHT:	6/6
SHOOT:	7/7
RESOLVE:	5
SPECIAL RULES:	Brawlers, Expert Artillery Crew, and Sailors

116

FRANCE

rench sea rovers were the first to singe the Spanish beard in the New World, and France has no intention of letting up. French adventurers showed up on Tortuga Island off the north coast of Hispaniola early in the seventeenth century. French hunters of cattle and swine soon came to be known as *boucaniers*, and just as soon were allied with French sea rovers, themselves soon to be known as *flibustiers*. These allies began with small forays against the Spanish, first from dugout canoes and piraguas, then later from larger vessels. Like the English, the French in the Caribbean, and especially on Saint-Domingue, as the French western part was known, came to rely on the flibustiers and boucaniers for defense, and almost thirty years longer. Although France at times agreed to reign in its Caribbean sea rovers, seldom did it stop supporting their plundering, whether by outright commission or via a "wink of the eye."

◊ FRENCH BUCCANEERS

They are easily identified, these adventurers, by their panache and silhouettes! They are unmistakable: the flibustiers with their plumes and sashes, their indigo-blue sackcloth coats, their monster-headed cutlasses and fusils boucaniers; the boucaniers with their bloody clothes, rude pig hock shoes, and fusils boucaniers; and the marins with their sashes, neckcloths, and rolling gaits. Like their English counterparts, these Gallic buccaneers are men of many nations, races, and ethnicities, even if predominantly French. Many of them are Huguenots, not Catholics, but even the latter will rob a Spanish church, yet save a bit of its plunder to give to the poor and to the small churches of Saint-Domingue. A fair portion of their most famous captains are Dutch, many of whom are as fond of *gasconades* and *fanfaronades* as are the colorful French themselves. They are expert shots, most of them, and as comfortable boarding a ship in action as they are storming a Spanish castle ashore. Their favored tactic at sea is boarding, and is much the same ashore: attack with musketry, run up under the enemy's walls, lob grenades over the walls . . . then enter and let the close combat begin!

FORCE SPECIAL RULES

» Once per game, this force's controlling player may discard all the Activation Cards in their hand and replace them with the same number of new cards without spending a Fortune Point.

» This force always adds +2 to its roll to determine attacker.

CORE UNITS

Flibustiers, Boucaniers, Marins

SUPPORT UNITS

Les Enfants Perdus, Freebooters

FORCE OPTIONS

OLD HANDS: All of the Flibustiers, Les Enfants Perdus and/or Boucaniers in this force may be upgraded from Trained to Veteran for 1 point per model.

GRAPESHOT: All cannons in this force may add Grapeshot (*see Equipment p.* 124) for free, but may fire using only Grapeshot for the duration of the battle.

◊ FLIBUSTIERS NAU

FORCE SPECIAL RULES

» Once per game, this force's controlling player may discard all the Activation Cards in their hand and replace them with the same number of new cards without spending a Fortune Point.

» All units in this force gain the Ruthless special rule.

» This force always adds +3 to its roll to determine attacker.

CORE UNITS

Flibustiers, Les Enfants Perdus

SUPPORT UNITS

Marins
Boucaniers

FORCE OPTIONS

OLD HANDS: All units of one type in this force may be upgraded from Trained to Veteran for 1 point per model.

FRENCH UNITS

◊ FLIBUSTIERS   ◊ BOUCANIERS

6 POINTS

Flibustiers are second only to the Boucaniers in experience in raiding Spanish ships and settlements. Like most French fighting men of their time, they preferred to quickly move into close action where they could quickly bring their braces of pistols to bear at point blank range.

EXPERIENCE LEVEL:	Trained
MAIN WEAPONS:	Buccaneer Guns, Brace of Pistols, Standard Melee Weapons
SIDE ARMS:	None
FIGHT:	5/7
SHOOT:	6/7
RESOLVE:	5
SPECIAL RULES:	Ball & Shot, Fast Reload, and Sailors

7 POINTS

The Boucaniers were the predecessors of both French Flibustiers and English Freebooters. Known for their deadly accuracy, these hunters of mainly French origin originated from the western end of Hispaniola and lived a rough backwoods life. It wasn't long before these enterprising woodsmen began attacking passing Spanish ships, usually from canoes and other small watercraft.

EXPERIENCE LEVEL:	Trained
MAIN WEAPONS:	Buccaneer Guns, Standard Melee Weapons
SIDE ARMS:	None
FIGHT:	7/7
SHOOT:	5/6
RESOLVE:	6
SPECIAL RULES:	Ball & Shot, Fast Reload, Elusive, and Marksmen

FRENCH UNITS

◇ LES ENFANTS PERDUS

◇ MARINS

6 POINTS

"The Lost Children" are an advanced raiding unit of the French buccaneer forces. These fearless Flibustiers earned their name because of the dangerous tasks they performed, like storming fortresses and ambushing superior enemy forces with explosives.

EXPERIENCE LEVEL:	Trained
MAIN WEAPONS:	Buccaneer Guns, Brace of Pistols Standard Melee Weapons
SIDE ARMS:	Explosives
FIGHT:	5/8
SHOOT:	6/8
RESOLVE:	4
SPECIAL RULES:	Ball & Shot, Fast Reload, Vanguard, and Tough

WEAPON OPTIONS: In a unit of Les Infants Perdus, one model in every four is also armed with a single type of Explosive (grenado, firepot, or stinkpot: controlling player's choice) as a Main Weapon for no additional cost. A unit which has multiple models with Explosives may select different types.

4 POINTS

French sailors had great experience in naval combat from their many engagements in Europe, the Mediterranean, and the Americas. Usually armed with a fine French pistol, they were known to excel at boarding actions.

EXPERIENCE LEVEL:	Trained
MAIN WEAPONS:	Pistol, Standard Melee Weapons
SIDE ARMS:	None
FIGHT:	5/7
SHOOT:	7/7
RESOLVE:	5
SPECIAL RULES:	Sailors, Artillery Crew, and Hard Chargers

UNAFFILIATED FACTIONS

◊ BRETHREN OF THE COAST

These adventurers are of all nations, races, and ethnicities, and their sole purpose is to harry Spain—to plunder the Spanish Main! They are English buccaneers, French flibustiers, Dutch freebooters, Spanish deserters, Portuguese seamen, and freed slaves and other men of color, all banded together for common purpose. If they are English and are forbidden to plunder the Spanish, they will accept a French commission, and if French and so forbidden, an English commission. And if there is no commission to be had, they will make a pretense of one and attack the Spanish anyway. They are naturally armed as are the English buccaneers and French flibustiers, both of whom are in their number: with flintlock musket (usually a fusil boucanier), cartouche box of thirty cartridges, a pistol or two, and a cutlass.

FORCE SPECIAL RULES

» Once per game, this force's controlling player may discard all the Activation Cards in their hand and replace them with the same number of new cards without spending a Fortune Point.

» This force always adds +2 to its roll to determine attacker.

CORE UNITS	SUPPORT UNITS
Flibustiers, Freebooters, Marins, Sea Dogs, Marineros	Boucaniers, Forlorn Hope OR Les Enfants Perdus (one, not both)

FORCE OPTIONS

VARIED EXPERIENCE: All Core units of one type may be upgraded one Experience Level for +1 point per model. All Core units of one type may be downgraded one Experience Level for -1 point per model.

GRAPESHOT: All cannons in this force may add Grapeshot (see Equipment) for free, but may fire using only Grapeshot for the duration of the battle (*p. 124*).

9.4 Aids for Purchasing and Outfitting Ships

TYPE	SLOOP	BRIGANTINE	LIGHT FRIGATE	LONGBOAT
Point cost	14	16	21	3
Top Speed	4"	4"	5"	4"
Windward	-0"	-1"	-2"	-1"
Turn	4"	3"	3"	3"
Draft	4	6	8	-
Size (Decks)	2	3	3	1
Cannons (Fore/Mid/Aft Deck)	6 (6/-/0)	8 (0/4/4)	14 (2/6/6*)	0
Swivels (Fore/Mid/Aft Deck)	6 (2/-/4)	6 (4/0/2)	4 (2/0/2)	1
Hull Fortitude	4	4	5	2
Hull Integrity	5	6	6	3
Rigging Fortitude	3	3	3	-
Rigging Integrity	4	5	6	-
Sail Settings	4"/2"/0"/A	4"/3"/2"/0"/A	5"/4"/3"/2"/0"/A	3"/0"/A
Traits	Sweeps:2 Simple Rig Fore-and-Aft Rig	Sweeps 2 Stay Sails Hybrid Rig	Stay Sails Chasers: 2 (stern)	Sweeps:4 Low Profile

* Two of the gun ports are "chasers" that face straight backward from the stern of the ship.

Table 5: *Ship Stat Summary*

9.5 Ship Traits

SWEEPS: X: May move up to X" under oars while sails are set at speed 0" and the Sweeps are crewed.

STAYSAILS: When moving under sail to windward, this ship is never reduced to less than its slowest Sail Setting value (unless it is In the Wind's Eye). Use of Staysails is optional.

CHASERS: Chasers are Cannons that face either forward out of the bow, or out back from the stern of the ship. If Cannons are placed in the Chasers gun ports, they may fire in the direction they face, with the width of the bow (or stern) as their Arc of Fire.

FORE-AND-AFT RIG: When this ship attempts a Tacking Advanced Maneuver, it may roll two d10 for the Test, and use the best result. This ship cannot perform the Box Hauling Advanced Maneuver.

HYBRID RIG: As long as this ship's sails are not at their highest setting, it gains the Fore-and-Aft Rig ship trait.

SIMPLE RIG: This ships Sail Setting may be changed using a Standard action instead of a Dedicated action. Additionally, apply a +1 penalty when taking a Shoot Test to hit this ship's Rigging.

LOW PROFILE: Apply a +4 penalty to a Shoot Test attempting to hit the Hull of this ship.

GUN TYPE	MINIMUM CREW	D10 ROLLED PER GUN	SHOOT TEST BASE NUMBER	RELOAD MARKERS GAINED AFTER FIRING	ARC OF FIRE ON SHIP	ARC OF FIRE ON FIELD CARRIAGE OR FORTIFICATION	MOVE PENALTY ON FIELD CARRIAGE	POINTS PER GUN (ON A STRUCTURE)	POINTS PER GUN (ON A FIELD CARRIAGE)
Swivel Gun	2	3 vs. Units & Rigging only	6	2	360°	360°	-1"	2	4
Light Cannon	2	1 (+2)	0	4	Width of deck	45° pivot	-1"	5	10
Medium Cannon	3	1 (+3)	0	4	Width of deck	45° pivot	-2"	7	14
Heavy Cannon	4	1 (+4)	0	4	Width of deck	45° pivot	immobile	9	18

* Artillery on a ship is purchased in pairs.

Table 4: *Artillery Stats Chart*

9.6 Special Rules

These are full descriptions of the Special Rules listed on each unit card. Special Rules that are exclusive to commanders are marked as such.

Remember, suit-activated abilities do not trigger if the unit activated is taking a Dedicated action, or if the unit is Shaken.

◊ ARTILLERY CREW

If this unit is activated with a ♠, it may take a free Reload action with Artillery that it is assigned to.

◊ BALL & SHOT

This unit loads small shot with regular musket balls to cause greater damage.

When this unit rolls any natural 10s for a Ranged attack using muskets against an enemy unit no more than 12" away, an additional d10 may be rolled for each natural 10 in an attempt to score additional hits. Natural 10s rolled with the bonus dice do not trigger any additional dice.

◊ BRAWLERS

This unit can roll an additional d10 for each natural 10 rolled during a Fight Test to attempt to score additional hits. Natural 10s rolled with the bonus dice do not trigger any additional rolls.

◊ BROADSIDE! (COMMANDER ONLY)

All Artillery fired during this commander's activation are fired simultaneously, hence it all counts as the same Ranged Attack, and all dice for the Shoot Test are rolled simultaneously. This may increase the chances of scoring Critical Hits.

◊ COMMODORE (COMMANDER ONLY)

When this commander is aboard a ship, its command range is increased by 12" when giving actions to units on other ships.

◊ DRILLED

This unit is more effective when in formation. A Drilled unit in formation may make a Shoot action as a Dedicated action, which receives all the standard penalties and bonuses for a Dedicated action as explained in the Actions section.

To be in formation this unit must:

» have at least 4 models

» not be Shaken

» have no models in a Structure, unless that Structure section is open-topped.

» have all models in base to base contact.

Units in formation still have a 360° Arc of Fire just as an individual model would.

Units don't need to move in formation, but they must be in formation at the end of a move to benefit from the Drilled skill.

◊ ELUSIVE

This unit may add a -1 bonus to its Ranged Saves if all of its models are in Cover (but not inside a Structure).

◊ EXPERT ARTILLERY CREW

If this unit is activated with a ♠ or ♥, it may take a free Reload action with Artillery that it is assigned to.

◊ EXPERTLY DRILLED

This unit has the Drilled Special Rule. In addition, if this unit Activates with a ♠ or ♥ and makes a successful Dedicated Shoot action with muskets while in formation, the defending unit must roll and additional d10 when taking its Fatigue Test from the attack.

◊ FAST RELOAD

If this unit is activated with a ♠ card, and it is not Engaged in a Melee Combat, it may immediately take a free Reload action with Small Arms.

◊ FIELD GUN

This unit may be deployed with a piece of Artillery on a field carriage. It must pay the points for the chosen Artillery piece (*see Table 4 p. 129*).

◊ HIGH STANDING (COMMANDER ONLY)

Due to physical limitations, inexperience, or arrogance, this commander does not move quickly or participate in acts of subterfuge.

When a commander with High Standing is attached to a unit with Elusive, Quick, Scout, or Skirmisher, that unit loses those Special Rules as long as the commander remains attached.

◊ GOD'S BLESSING OR THE DEVILS' LUCK (COMMANDER ONLY)

A force led by this commander starts the game with 4 Fortune Points.

◊ HARD CHARGERS

When charging, this unit receives a -1 bonus to the Fight Test for the free Fight action.

◊ INSPIRING (COMMANDER ONLY)

All friendly units within the Command Range of this commander may reroll any failed Rally test results when the commander's unit is active.

◊ LEAD BY EXAMPLE (COMMANDER ONLY)

If the unit that includes this commander causes an opposing unit to be removed from the game (either as casualties or by routing), all units in this commander's force may remove a point of Fatigue.

◊ LUCKY (COMMANDER ONLY)

Any time this commander's force uses a Fortune Point for a re-roll, the Fortune Point is not spent if the result of the re-roll is not better than the original roll.

◊ MARKSMEN

This unit may spend 2 actions to make a Shoot Test with any musket or carbine at a -1 bonus. A player must declare this before rolling the Shoot Test.

◊ POORLY EQUIPPED

If this unit is activated by a ♣, it gains one additional Reload marker to Small Arms or Artillery if it gains any during that activation.

◊ QUICK

If this unit is activated with a ♠ card, and it is not Engaged in a Melee Combat, it may immediately take a free Move action.

◊ RUTHLESS

This unit receives a -1 bonus to Shoot Tests with Small Arms (but not Explosives), and to Fight Tests against units with more Fatigue than this unit.

If a unit with Ruthless makes a Ranged Attack into Structure section with two enemy units, the Ruthless bonus is determined for both units using the enemy unit in the section with the greatest amount of Fatigue.

This is also the case if a Ruthless unit is engaged in Melee combat with multiple enemy units.

◊ SAILORS

A unit with this special rule can pass ship Advanced Maneuver and Sail Setting Tests on a 5+.

◊ SCOUTS

This unit may move through rough area terrain (not inside Structures, and not while climbing) without the -1" movement penalty.

◊ SKIRMISHERS

When this unit is activated with a ♠ or a ♥ card:

> » If the unit takes a Move action then attempts one or more Ranged Attacks, it may take a free Move action back to its original position after the Ranged Attacks are resolved.

> » If the unit Charges an enemy unit, it may take a free Move action back to its original position after the Charge Fight action resolved. In this case. the enemy unit cannot pursue the Skirmisher unit.

◊ TIMID

If a friendly unit within 5" of this unit takes any Casualties, this unit must roll a Fatigue Test on a single d10.

◊ TOUGH

If this unit ends an activation with any amount of Fatigue, and it did not Push, it may remove a point of Fatigue at the end of its activation.

◊ VANGUARD

This unit may take a free Move Action on the first turn of a game, at the beginning of the Start Phase before cards are drawn. If multiple forces have this rule, the attacker moves their units with Vanguard first.

◊ VERY INSPIRING (COMMANDER ONLY)

All friendly units within the Command Range of this commander may re-roll any failed Rally test results.

◊ WELL EQUIPPED (COMMANDER ONLY)

If this commander is attached to a unit with the Poorly Equipped special rule, it is negated.

9.7 *Equipment*

◊ HORSE

A model with a horse is considered to start the game Mounted. A horse and its rider are considered to be one model, and are not targeted separately.

The bonuses:

» Mounted units may take a free Move action during their activation.

» Mounted units may use Move actions while engaged in Melee Combat to voluntarily leave the Melee. Treat this exactly like a Shaken unit fleeing Melee Combat (Step 5 of Initiating Melee Combat), except the enemy unit cannot pursue the Mounted unit.

» A Defensive Attack taken against a Mounted unit gets a +1 penalty to the Shoot Test.

All models in the unit must be Mounted to receive the bonuses listed above.

The penalties:

» Mounted units have an additional -1" to Move actions in Rough terrain.

» Mounted units may not enter Structures.

» Mounted units may not climb terrain.

» Mounted units cannot shoot with muskets of any type.

A unit may dismount anytime by taking a Dismount action to replace the mounted model with the appropriate model on foot. If an appropriate model on foot is not available, the model may not dismount. Once a unit has dismounted, it must remain that way for the rest of the battle.

◊ TORCHES

Torches increase a unit's chances to start Structures on fire, but make them very easy to spot at night.

» Any unit that is not Mounted may take Torches for 3 points.

» Carrying Torches does not affect the movement or combat ability of the unit in any way.

» A unit with Torches receives a -2 bonus to the Start Fire action.

» A unit with Torches (and anything within 6" of that unit) is visible from any distance in a scenario that takes place at night (taking normal Line of Sight rules into account, or course).

» A unit with lit Torches may not take them on a ship or in any other Structure unless they intend to set it on fire (it's too dangerous).

» Units with Torches always count as having them (down to the last model in a unit), unless the unit wishes to extinguish them. A unit can extinguish its Torches during its activation without spending an action, but the torch bonus is lost for the rest of the battle.

◊ GRAPESHOT

Grapeshot is a type of anti-personnel ammunition that can be purchased for Cannons. It has a short range and cannot damage a ship's Hull, but it can inflict horrendous damage on a ship's crew.

» Grapeshot costs 1 point for each Cannon on a field carriage, or one point for every pair of Cannons on a ship. Every Cannon in a unit or pair a ship must be counted and paid for when outfitting with Grapeshot, and every Cannon in that unit or on that ship counts as having it.

» Right before a Cannon with Grapeshot is fired, the controlling player has the option of using it instead of firing the gun normally (as explained under Making a Ranged Attack with Artillery).

» Grapeshot allows the Cannon to fire similar to a Swivel Gun:

• Cannons firing Grapeshot have a base target number of 6+ for Shoot Tests.

• Each Cannon firing Grapeshot rolls its total number of dice for the Shoot Test simultaneously (for example, a Medium Cannon firing Grapeshot would roll 4 d10).

• Cannons firing Grapeshot target units in the manner of Small Arms, not Artillery. Therefore, they may only target units, units inside Structures, and ship's Rigging.

• Cannons firing Grapeshot do not roll additional dice for extra hits against units like Cannons do.

• The Arc of Fire of a Cannon firing Grapeshot does not change.

• A Cannon firing Grapeshot gains 4 Reload markers as usual.

• Cannons firing Grapeshot cannot be used to make Defensive Attacks when charged.

10

Fortune

ortune represents the skill, luck, and influence of a force.

Every force begins the game with 3 Fortune points by default (though certain characters may increase or decrease that amount). Fortune is not replenished in the course of a game.

A player may spend one Fortune point at any time to do any one of the following:

» RE-ROLL: A player may re-roll all the dice for one Test or another roll that they are attempting, immediately after the original roll is made. The new results are final, even if they are worse than the original result. (Remember, any roll in Blood & Plunder may be re-rolled only once).

» MULLIGAN: Discard any number of Activation Cards in your hand and draw new cards to replace them. This may be done at any point in the turn.

» CHEAT DEATH: If your force's commander is alone or would be removed as a Casualty, and there is a friendly unit within 8", you may immediately move the commander to join the new unit. This may be done regardless of the type of unit, and even if the new unit is separated by impassable terrain.

II
Events

vents are immediately triggered when a Joker is drawn from a player's deck of Activation Cards. When this happens, the player rolls on the table below to determine the effect. If both players draw a Joker at the same time, randomly determine who resolves their Event first.

Events are not mandatory for play. If you would prefer to not play with Events, all players should ignore any Jokers when drawn, and draw another card in its place.

II.1 *Event Table*

D10 ROLL	RESULT
1	**MISFORTUNE** » A random unit, determined amongst all forces, either gains 2 Fatigue or gains 3 Reload markers on their Main Weapons (or Artillery, if crewing a gun). The choice is up to the player who controls the unit. » A unit that cannot gain Reload markers (such as units armed with Bows or a Brace of Pistols) must take the 2 Fatigue points instead. **AND** **WIND CHANGE** » Roll once on the Wind Table.
2	**CONFUSION** » The player that drew this Event card does not replace it with another from their deck.
3	**STUBBORN** » The player that drew this Event card picks a unit their force, and removes 1 Fatigue point from it.
4	**UNRULY** » The force of the player that drew the Event card immediately loses a Command Point for this turn only.
5–6	**WEATHER CHANGE** » Roll once on the Weather Table. **AND** **WIND CHANGE** » Roll once on the Wind Table.
7	**LUCKY** » The player that drew this Event Card picks a unit in their force at random. That unit can take a free action of its choice this turn.
8	**INSPIRING COMMAND** » The force of the player that drew the Event card immediately gains a Command Point for the remainder of this turn only.
9	**EXHAUSTED** » The player that drew this Event Card picks a unit in their force at random. That unit immediately gains a point of Fatigue.
10	**TWIST OF FATE** » All players discard their hands into their discard piles, then remove any number of discarded cards of the player's choice (including all played Event cards) from the game. Players then shuffle their discard piles into their decks, and redraw their hands. **AND** **WIND CHANGE** » Roll once on the Wind Table.

◊ WIND

Scenarios start at 0 Wind speed unless otherwise noted. The minimum and maximum wind speeds are -2/+2 (although a Lull and a Gust can push it as high as -3/+3 for a turn)

Wind effects last until they are changed by another result rolled on the table. Wind direction can change without affecting Wind speed, and vice versa.

Wind speed typically has no effect on gameplay unless ships are involved.

D10 ROLL	WIND RESULT
1	No change in Wind
2	Wind direction shifts one table edge clockwise
3	Wind direction shifts one table edge counterclockwise
4	No change in Wind
5	Wind speed +1
6	Wind speed -1
7	Lull (Wind speed -1 for this turn only)
8	Gust (Wind speed +1 for this turn only)
9	Player that drew event picks a Wind event on this table
10	Opponent picks a Wind event on this table

◊ WEATHER

Scenarios start at the 0 space (Fair) on the Weather Chart unless otherwise noted.

The weather effect applies until another roll on the Weather Table changes it (for better or worse).

If the battle is taking place at night, any negative results rolled on the Weather table are not applied below 0. (It can't be blazingly hot if the sun's not up!

D10 ROLL	WEATHER RESULT
1–4	-1 on the Weather Effects Chart
5–6	No Change
7–10	+1 on the Weather Effects Chart

Weather Table

SWELTERING

-3

» Units using Small Arms have a +1 penalty to any Ranged Attack attempted at a range of greater than 20".

» Any unit that moves more than 4" a turn (instead of the normal 8") gains a Fatigue point.

» All models that participate in a Melee Combat (and survive) during Sweltering Heat gain +1 Fatigue (on top of any other Fatigue) as a result of the Melee Combat.

HOT

2

» Units using Small Arms have a +1 penalty to any Ranged Attack attempted at a range of greater than 20".

» Any unit that moves more than 4" a turn (instead of the normal 8") gains a Fatigue point.

BLINDING SUN

-1

» Units using Small Arms have a +1 penalty to any Ranged Attack attempted at a range of greater than 20".

FAIR

0

» No effect on gameplay.

LIGHT RAIN

+1

» Limited visibility of 28"

» Any unit that takes a Shoot Action that is not inside a Structure with a roof gains an additional Reload marker.

HEAVY RAIN

+2

» Limited visibility of 20"

» All Move actions have a -1" penalty

» Any unit that takes a Shoot Action that is not inside a Structure with a roof gains 2 additional Reload markers.

TORRENTIAL DOWNPOUR

+3

» Limited visibility of 12"

» All Move Action have a -1" penalty

» Ranged Attacks are impossible in a Torrential Downpour.

12
Scenarios

nce both players have spent their points and built their forces, the last step is to set up a table and play a game!

The following section explains how to set up the game board and how to play different scenarios. Optional rules are also included to add variety and replayability.

12.1 *Game Setup Basics*

All the criteria below are based on a standard two player game.

1. PICK GAME TYPE

Before a game table is set up, players decide the type of game they are playing based on the composition of their forces:

> » A **land battle** requires that no players have ships in their forces.

> » An **amphibious battle** (ship-to-shore) battle is possible if one or both players have ships in their forces.

> » A **sea battle** is only possible if all players have ships in their forces that can carry all of their units.

2. DETERMINE MINIMUM BOARD SIZE

◊ FOR A LAND BATTLE USE AT LEAST:

> » a 3' wide by 3' long board for battles less than 200 points per player.

> » a 3' wide by 4' long board for battles from 201–300 points per player.

> » a 3' wide by 5' long board for battles from 301+ points per player.

◊ FOR SEA AND AMPHIBIOUS BATTLES, USE AT LEAST:

> » a 3' wide by 4' long board for battles less than 200 points per player.

> » a 4' wide by 4' long board for battles from 201–300 points per player.

> » a 4' wide by 6' long board for battles from 301+ points per player.

For amphibious battles, at least 25 percent of the area should be navigable water so ships can maneuver (or the percent suggested in the scenario description). Some of this water area must include one or both of the player's deployment zones. Oftentimes this represented by one or more islands, a peninsula, or a shoreline along one side of the board.

For a sea battle, the entire area of the board should be water, with the majority of it navigable. It is also a good idea to play on a surface larger than the recommended size when playing a sea battle to prevent having to scroll the table and provide more room for maneuvering. When doing so, the deployment areas should be centered on the board using the recommended sizes.

3. CHOOSE SCENARIO

It is a good idea to roll or pick the scenario you plan to play at this point, if you haven't already done so when building a force. This will make it easier to set up the terrain in the next step.

4. SET UP THE GAME BOARD

First, make sure that the arrangement and ratio of land to water is agreeable to both players. Once this is decided, place any terrain elements that are integral to the scenario you are playing, such as mission objectives or structures.

Some mission objectives are better placed after the board is fully set up. This is fine as well.

After the terrain that is important to the scenario has been placed on the board, players mutually decide how much other terrain they would like to place on the board.

Players may add as little or as much terrain as they would like, but generally:

> » Land and amphibious battles benefit from more terrain, as it provides more cover to units. We would suggest covering at least a third of the board with terrain that provides Cover, including a few pieces that can block Line of Sight.

> » Sea battles benefit from less terrain, as it gives ships more room to maneuver without worrying about collisions or running aground.

> » Terrain should be a mix of different types, if possible. Different elevations of terrain will add some excellent tactical variety as well.

Once they players have decided on the amount and type of terrain, both players take turns placing it on the board in whatever arrangement they desire. Once all the terrain has been placed, both players must agree on the layout before the game can progress.

If a scenario does not dictate which way the wind is blowing, and wind direction is necessary (such as for an amphibious engagement), randomly determine which table edge the wind is blowing from at this point.

ROLL	1–2	3–4	5–6	7–8	9	10
Wind Direction	North	East	South	West	Defender's choice	Attacker's choice

5. DETERMINE ATTACKER & DEFENDER

Both players roll one d10 to determine attacker and defender. The higher roll is the attacker; the lower roll is the defender. (Remember, some forces have a modifier to the attacker/defender roll). Re-roll any ties.

> » The defender chooses a valid deployment zone as described by the chosen scenario, and places a unit first unless the scenario states otherwise. Ships are deployed before any units, and may be placed facing any direction unless dictated otherwise by the scenario.

> » The attacker then deploys a unit in the other deployment zone with any ships placed first. Ships may be placed facing in any direction unless dictated otherwise by the scenario.

> » The ship that contains a force's commander at the start of the battle is considered the force's flagship, and may be important in certain scenarios. A flagship may not be a boat unless that force does not contain a ship with two or more decks.

> » The attacker and defender alternate placing units in their deployment zones until both players are out of units to deploy.

6. PLACE UNITS & START GAME

Once all units have been deployed, the first turn of the game starts.

12.2 *Strike Points and Strike Tests*

Battles in this era were very rarely fought to the last man, and forces often capitulated before their losses were too great. In Blood & Plunder, forces must take a Strike Test when things start looking grim to see if they've got the courage to stay in the fight.

Throughout a game a force can earn Strike Points as it takes Casualties and loses advantage. Each force checks for Strike Points at the end of each turn.

A force will gain a Strike Point when (if at the end of a turn):

> » The force has lost 25 percent of its starting models as Casualties (one Strike Point for each 25 percent).

> » One of the force's ships suffers a Catastrophic Damage Critical Damage result.

» A deck on a force's flagship is currently occupied by at least 1 enemy unit. (The flagship is the one that the commander starts the battle on.)

» The Fortitude value of the Hull or Rigging of force's flagship has been reduced to half its starting value (rounded down).

» One of the force's ships (not boats) has been immobilized by Critical Damage or Running Aground.

» One of the force's ships (not boats) has been lost (by capture, fire, or sinking).

» The enemy force fulfills an objective requirement for the Scenario being played.

Strike Points are cumulative and are determined at the end of each turn.

If any force has two more Strike Points than the opposing force at the end of a turn, that player's force must immediately roll a Strike Test. Roll one d10, with the Resolve of the force's commander as the target number. If successful, the game moves on to the next turn. Otherwise, the force surrenders and the opponent claims victory!

If a force's commander has been removed as a Casualty, the force automatically fails any Strike Test it may have to make.

NO QUARTER!

If both players agree, the game can be played without Strike Tests. Strike Points are still tracked to determine the winner at the end of the scenario's turn limit.

DETERMINING THE VICTOR

A game will continue until one force has failed a Strike Test, or the game has reached its pre established turn limit. If neither force has failed a Strike Test before the end of the game, the player with the fewest Strike Points wins.

If there is a tie, each player adds up the total point cost of all their models removed as Casualties. The player who lost the fewest total points' worth of models is then declared the winner. If there is still a tie, the game is considered a draw.

12.3 *Game Scenarios*

All deployment zones for the land scenarios below are scaled to a 3' x 4' game board. Amphibious and sea scenarios are scaled to a 4' x 4' board. Adjust the measurements accordingly based on the size of the board you are playing on.

Each of the scenarios below have a land, amphibious, and sea option. Players may pick the scenario they would like to play, or roll 1 d10 to randomly determine the scenario.

1–2 BREAKTHROUGH

The attacker tries to push deeper into enemy territory. The defender must stop them!

◊ LAND

SETUP:

The entire board is land terrain, but no specific terrain set up is required.

DEPLOYMENT:

Defending player chooses one board edge; the attacker takes the opposite.

It is suggested that the defender's deployment zone is measured and marked at the board edge to determine if the scenario objectives have been met (see below).

GAME LENGTH:

Six turns

OBJECTIVES:

» Defender gains a Strike Point if the attacker has a unit completely in their deployment zone.

» Attacker gains a Strike Point if the attacker has no units within 4" of the defender's deployment zone by the end of turn 3 or later.

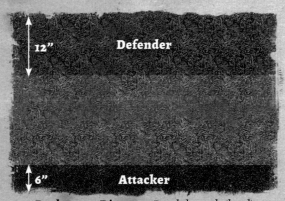

Deployment Diagram: *Breakthrough (land)*

◊ AMPHIBIOUS

SETUP:

One side of the board must have a land mass that takes up 25 to 50 percent of the board area and does not extend past the centerline of the board (see diagram). The rest of the board is navigable water. Players determine if there is any water terrain (such as Shoals) and define the areas of Shoreline.

SCENARIO RULES:

The attacking force must have models on the land portion of the board at the end of turn 3 or later, or that force gains a Strike Point.

DEPLOYMENT:

The defending force sets up on the land side of the board, the attacker comes in from the sea on the opposite side.

Determine the wind direction randomly before any ships are placed.

It is suggested that the defender's deployment zone is measured and marked at the board edge to determine if the scenario objectives have been met *(see below)*.

GAME LENGTH:

Six turns

OBJECTIVES:

» Defender gains a Strike Point if the attacker has a unit completely in their deployment zone.

» Attacker gains a Strike Point if the attacker has no units within 4" of the defender's deployment zone by the end of turn 3 or later.

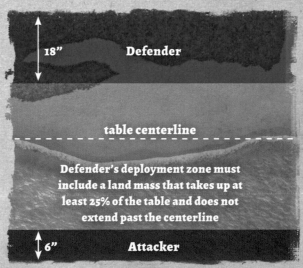

Deployment Diagram: *Breakthrough (amphibious)*

◊ SEA

SETUP:

The whole board is considered Deep Water, with any additional water terrain added at the discretion of the players. The defender's board edge is considered impassable and blocks all movement (this represents a stretch of coastline that the defender's ship is trapped against).

DEPLOYMENT:

The defending force sets up within 6" of the impassable edge, the attacker sets up anywhere else at least 24" away from the defender. The attacker may not set up with the bow of any of their ships pointed windward (but boats may be).

GAME LENGTH:

Six turns

OBJECTIVES:

> » Defender gains a Strike Point at the end of turn 3 or later if the attacker is within 8" of the defender's flagship.

> » Attacker gains a Strike Point if the defender's flagship is not within 12" of the attacker at the end of turn 3 or later.

> » Attacker/Defender: If an opponent's flagship is reduced to at least half its Top Speed due to Rigging damage at the end of any turn, that player gains a Strike Point.

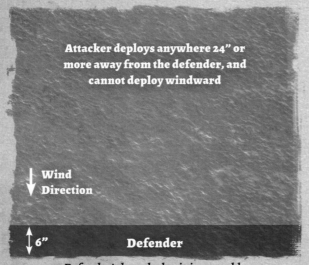

Attacker deploys anywhere 24" or more away from the defender, and cannot deploy windward

Wind Direction

6" Defender

Defender's board edge is impassable

Deployment Diagram: *Breakthrough (sea)*

3–4 RAID

The defender is protecting a stockpile of supplies or valuables. The attacker must drive them off to capture their vessel or secure the loot!

◊ LAND

SETUP:

The entire board is land terrain, but no specific terrain set up is required.

DEPLOYMENT:

The defending player chooses one board quadrant. The attacker will deploy within 6" of the opposite board edges *(see diagram)*.

Before any units are placed, the defender places one objective marker (representing loot) within their deployment zone. The attacker than places another objective marker in the defender's deployment zone. The two markers must be at least 10" apart, neither can be within 4" of a board edge, and neither marker can be in impassable terrain.

GAME LENGTH:

Six turns

OBJECTIVES:

> » Defender gains a Strike Point if the attacker has a unit that is not Shaken within 4" of any objective marker and the defender has no units that are not Shaken within 4" of the same marker.

> » Attacker gains a Strike Point if they have no units within 4" of an objective marker at the end of turn 3 or later.

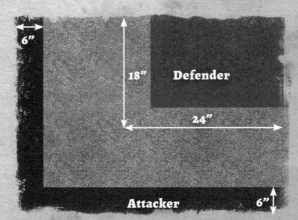

6"

18" Defender

24"

Attacker 6"

Deployment Diagram: *Raid (land)*

◊ AMPHIBIOUS

SETUP:

One side of the board must have a land mass that takes up 25 to 50 percent of the board area and does not extend past the centerline of the board (see diagram). The rest of the board is navigable water. Players determine if there is any water terrain (such as Shoals) and define the areas of Shoreline.

SCENARIO RULES:

The attacking force must have models on the land portion of the board at the end of turn 3 or later, or that force gains a Strike Point.

DEPLOYMENT:

The defending player chooses one board quadrant containing a land mass. The attacker will deploy ships on the opposite board edges (see diagram).

Before any units are placed, the defender places one objective marker (representing loot) within their deployment zone. The attacker than places another objective marker in the defender's deployment zone. The two markers must be at least 10" apart, neither can be within 6" of a board edge, and neither marker can be in impassable or Deep Water terrain.

Determine the wind direction randomly before any ships are placed. The attacker's ships must be placed so part of the ship is within 2" of the board edge.

GAME LENGTH:

Six turns

OBJECTIVES:

» Defender gains a Strike Point if the attacker has a unit that is not Shaken within 4" of any objective marker and the defender has no units that are not Shaken within 4" of the same marker.

» Attacker gains a Strike Point if they have no units within 4" of an objective marker at the end of turn 3 or later.

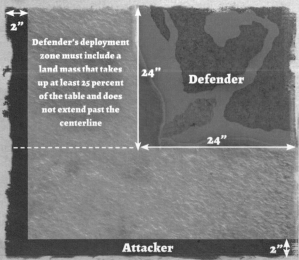

Deployment Diagram: *Raid (Amphibious)*

◊ SEA

SETUP:

The whole board is considered Deep Water, with any additional water terrain added at the discretion of the players.

DEPLOYMENT:

The defending force picks a board edge, and sets up ships so a part of the ship is within 2" of their deployment edge.

The attacker sets up anywhere else at least 24" away from the defender.

GAME LENGTH:

Six turns

OBJECTIVES:

» The Defender gain a Strike Point if the attacker captures the defender's flagship by the end of turn 6.

» The Attacker gains a Strike Point if the defender's flagship has not been captured by the end of turn 6.

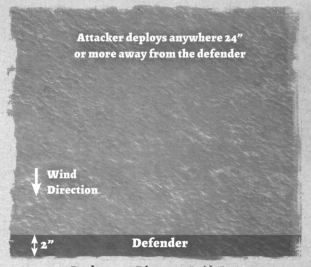

Deployment Diagram: *Raid (Sea)*

5–6 CONTROL THE FIELD

One force is attempting to outmaneuver the other in order to gain the advantage and drive off their foe.

◊ LAND

SETUP:

The entire board is land terrain, but no specific terrain set up is required.

DEPLOYMENT:

The defending player chooses one board corner. The attacker will deploy in the opposite board corner (*see diagram*).

Before any units are placed, an objective marker is placed in the center of the board. Two more markers are placed, each 12" away on either side of the central marker along the centerline of the board (*see diagram*). No markers can be placed in impassable terrain.

GAME LENGTH:

Six turns

OBJECTIVES:

» Attacker/Defender: A force gains a Strike Point if the enemy force has units that are not Shaken within 4" of any two objective markers and that force has no units that are not Shaken within 4" of the same markers.

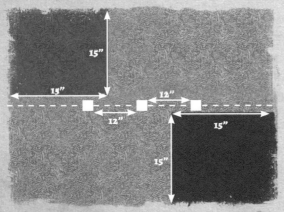

Deployment Diagram: *Control the Field (land)*

◊ AMPHIBIOUS

SETUP:

The center of the board must have a land mass that takes up 25 to 50 percent of the board area that encompasses the centerline of the board (see diagram). It may run to a board edge on one or both ends, or may be an island.

The rest of the board is navigable water. Players determine if there is any water terrain (such as Shoals) and define the areas of Shoreline.

SCENARIO RULES:

The attacking force must have models on the land portion of the board at the end of turn 3 or later, or that force gains a Strike Point.

DEPLOYMENT:

The defending player chooses one board side. The attacker will deploy in the opposite board side (see diagram).

Before any units are placed, an objective marker is placed in the center of the board. Two more markers are placed, each 12" away on either side of the central marker along the centerline of the board (see diagram). No markers can be placed in Impassable or Deep Water terrain.

Determine the wind direction randomly before any ships are placed. The attacker's ships must have a part of the ship within 3" of the board edge (but not the whole ship).

GAME LENGTH:

Six turns

OBJECTIVES:

» Attacker/Defender: A force gains a Strike Point if the enemy force has units that are not Shaken within 4" of any two objective markers and that force has no units that are not Shaken within 4" of the same markers.

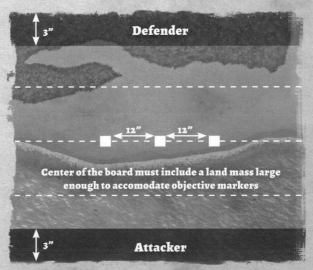

Deployment Diagram: *Control the Field (amphibious)*

◊ SEA

SETUP:

The whole board is considered Deep Water, with any additional water terrain added at the discretion of the players.

DEPLOYMENT:

The defending force picks a board edge, and sets up ships so a part of the ship is within 2" of their deployment edge.

The attacker sets up anywhere else at least 24" away from the defender.

GAME LENGTH:

Six turns

OBJECTIVES:

> » In this scenario, players attempt to control the weather gauge. In nautical terms, if you had the weather gauge it meant you were at tactical advantage because you were upwind of your opponent.

> » If the attacker's flagship is upwind of the defender's flagship at the end of turn 6, the defender gains a Strike Point.

> » If the defender's flagship is upwind of the attacker's flagship at the end of any turn, the attacker gains a Strike Point.

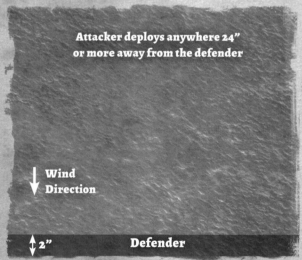

Deployment Diagram: *Control the Field (sea)*

7–8 TAKE AND HOLD

Both attacker and defender are attempting to control the battlefield by holding a crucial point on the battlefield such a hill, a beach, or the sea itself!

◊ LAND

SETUP:

The entire board is land terrain. An area of elevated terrain, a group of objects, or a Structure must be placed in the center of the table.

DEPLOYMENT:

Defending player chooses one board edge; the attacker takes the other.

Before any units are placed, an objective marker is placed in the center of the board in whatever terrain that was placed there during set up.

GAME LENGTH:

Six turns

OBJECTIVES:

> » Attacker/Defender: At the end of turn 3 or later, a force gains a Strike Point if the enemy force has a unit that is not Shaken within 4" of the objective marker and that force has no units that are not Shaken within 4" of the marker.

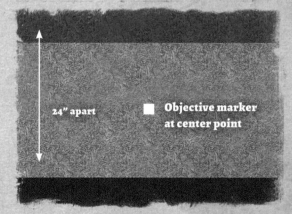

Deployment Diagram: *Take and Hold (land)*

◊ AMPHIBIOUS

SETUP:

One side of the board must have a land mass that takes up about 50 percent of the board area and includes the center point of the board (see diagram). The rest of the board is navigable water. Players determine if there is any water terrain (such as Shoals) and define the areas of Shoreline.

An area of terrain, a group of objects, or a Structure must be placed in the center of the table.

DEPLOYMENT:

The defending force sets up on the land side of the board, the attacker comes in from the sea (on the opposite side).

Before any units are placed, an objective marker is placed in the center of the board in whatever terrain that was placed there during set up.

Determine the wind direction randomly before any ships are placed.

Defender and attacker set up their forces at least 20" away from the objective marker at the center point.

GAME LENGTH:

Six turns

OBJECTIVES:

» Attacker/Defender: A force gains a Strike Point if the enemy force has a unit that is not Shaken within 4" of the objective marker and that force has no units that are not Shaken within 4" of the marker.

◊ SEA

SETUP:

The whole board is considered Deep Water, with any additional water terrain added at the discretion of the players.

DEPLOYMENT:

The defender sets up within 12" of a board edge facing in the wind direction. The attacker sets up the same way on the opposite board edge, at least 24" away from the defender (see diagram).

GAME LENGTH:

Six turns

OBJECTIVES:

» Attacker/Defender: A force that has its flagship captured immediately loses. In other words, the game will immediately end with the capturing force as the victor, regardless of Strike Points or any other factors.

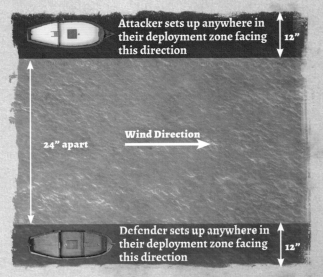

Deployment Diagram: *Take and Hold (sea)*

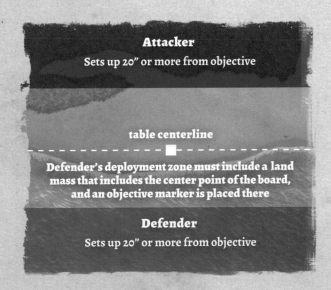

Deployment Diagram: *Take and Hold (amphibious)*

9–10   ENCOUNTER

Two opposing forces unexpectedly encounter each other while patrolling. Both sides wish to inflict as much damage to the enemy as possible.

◊ LAND

SETUP:

The entire board is land terrain, but no specific terrain set up is required.

DEPLOYMENT:

The defending player chooses one board corner. The attacker will deploy in the opposite board corner (see diagram).

GAME LENGTH:

Six turns

OBJECTIVES:

» None. Use the standard rules for Strike Points, and inflict the most harm to your foe!

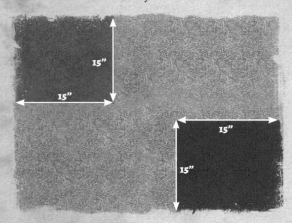

Deployment Diagram: *Encounter (land)*

◊ AMPHIBIOUS

SETUP:

One side of the board must have a land mass that takes up 25 to 75 percent of the board area. The rest of the board is navigable water. Players determine if there is any water terrain (such as Shoals) and define the areas of Shoreline.

SCENARIO RULES:

The attacking force must have models on the land portion of the board at the end of turn 3 or later, or that force gains a Strike Point.

DEPLOYMENT:

The defending player chooses one board corner with a land mass. The attacker will deploy in the opposite board corner which should have water to accommodate ships (see diagram).

Determine the wind direction randomly before any ships are placed.

GAME LENGTH:

Six turns

OBJECTIVES:

» None. Use the standard rules for Strike Points, and inflict the most harm to your foe!

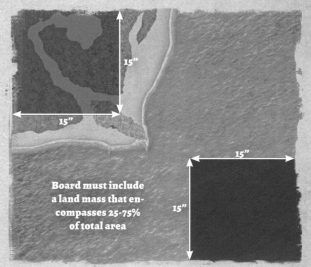

Deployment Diagram: *Encounter (amphibious)*

◊ SEA

SETUP:

The whole board is considered Deep Water, with any additional water terrain added at the discretion of the players.

DEPLOYMENT:

The defending force picks a board edge, and sets up at least 16" away from each corner, Ships are placed so a part of the ship is within 2" of their deployment edge (see diagram).

The attacker does the same on the opposite board edge.

All ships must be 90° to the wind (Abeam) when placed.

GAME LENGTH:

ix turns

OBJECTIVES:

> » None. Use the standard rules for Strike Points, and inflict the most harm to your foe!

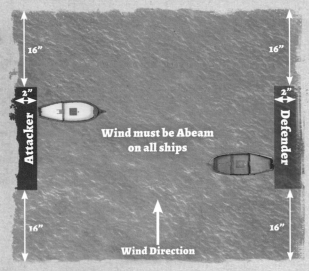

Deployment Diagram: Encounter (Sea)

12.4 *Create Your Own Scenarios*

The scenarios above are presented so you can set them up easily and start play quickly. They are not cast in stone, however. Players are encouraged to modify them in any way they would like. The Scenario Special Rules presented below are a great way to start, and represent battlefield conditions that can really influence the outcome of a battle. (A Raid is one thing, a Raid at night against a Drunk defender that is Caught Unaware is something completely different!)

Beyond that, players are encouraged to create their own scenarios from scratch. Feel free to borrow from the scenarios presented here, or come up with completely original stuff. If you come up with something that you're proud of, we would love to hear about it! Please post your ideas and original scenarios on the Firelock Games forum for all to see!

SCENARIO SPECIAL RULES

The special rules listed below are optional rules that you may add to any scenario. They are designed to add some theme and variety to an otherwise routine game of Blood & Plunder. All players must agree for a scenario special rule to be added to a game.

Players may use as many of these rules as they would like, but please note that the complexity increases with each rule that is added.

◊ CAUGHT UNAWARE

A force that is Caught Unaware is busy doing something else (like sleeping, training, or drinking heavily) and has no idea that an attacking force is dangerously close. This scenario rule is typically used in conjunction with Limited Visibility.

When using this rule, the one that is Caught Unaware (usually the defending force) sets up all its units first (except for ones held in reserve, see Reserves below).

Set up the units in the deployment zone as indicated by the Scenario, but units should be placed in buildings, in fields of crops, or in some other symbolic configuration to indicate that they are busy with other duties.

Then the defender sets up Sentries.

The defender receives 1 Sentry model for every 50 points in their force.

» Sentries are free; they do not count against the defender's point limit, and they do not count as being part of a unit.

» Sentries all have identical stats, each equivalent to a single model of a Core Unit of the defending player's choice.

All Sentries are set up outside of (but within 2") of the edge of the defender's deployment zone. All Sentries must be at least 9" apart from each other when they are placed on the board.

The Attacker sets up all his units (except for those that may be in reserve) as dictated by the Scenario.

After Activation Cards have been drawn, but before any have been played, both players resolve the movement of the Sentries:

» A Sentry that has not moved is nominated, and both players roll a d10.

» The player that rolls highest moves that Sentry 4" in any direction, following all the usual rules for movement. That Sentry must move as far as it can; it cannot remain in place.

» Repeat this process for each Sentry that has not moved.

After all the Sentries have moved, the attacking player may play cards to activate units as normal. The defending player may not, unless the alarm has been sounded (see below).

◊ SOUNDING THE ALARM

» If an attacking unit begins or ends an activation in Line of Sight to a Sentry, the alarm is sounded.

» If the attacker rolls a Shoot Test for any ranged weapon aside from Bows, the alarm is sounded.

» If a Sentry ends a movement within 4" (or Line of Sight, whichever is shorter) of the body of a Sentry, the alarm is sounded. (See Killing Sentries below).

» If an attacking unit has initiated a Melee Combat with an enemy unit (not a Sentry), the alarm is sounded.

» If the attacking force's commander uses a Command Point to give an action to a unit that is more than 4" away, the alarm is sounded.

When the alarm has been sounded for any reason, remove all Sentries from the board, and the defending player is free to activate his units as usual, starting on the next Initiative Step.

◊ KILLING SENTRIES

If a Sentry is killed, either by Bows or in Melee Combat, there is a chance it will go unnoticed. Roll a d10. On a 6+

the demise of the Sentry goes undetected, otherwise the alarm is raised.

If a Sentry is attacked and survives, the alarm is sounded.

When a Sentry is killed, leave its model face-down on the board to indicate the dead body. This is important in case another Sentry stumbles across it (see Sounding the Alarm above).

◊ DISTRACTION

A force causes a Distraction at the beginning of a battle, such as setting off an explosion or sending civilians into a panic. This may cause the opposing force to react until they realize it's a ruse.

The player who can cause a Distraction picks a unit that they control that will cause it. That unit:

» must begin the battle on the board,

» must be the first unit activated for that force, and

» the Distraction must be performed as a Dedicated action on the first turn of the game.

After a Distraction occurs, the player who did not cause the Distraction must roll a Resolve Test (1 d10) whenever one of their units activates during the first turn.

» If the Test is passed, the activated unit may take actions normally.

» If the Test is failed, the activated unit must use Move actions to move up to 8" toward the unit causing the Distraction, in as straight a line as possible. Any remaining actions are lost.

After the first turn of the game, the Distraction is determined to be a ruse, and units are activated and moved as normal.

◊ DRUNK

One (or both!) of the forces have been drinking heavily before the start of the battle. Though the units affected are much braver as a result, they are also clumsy and reckless.

Each force that is Drunk rolls a d10 for each of their units. On a 5+, that unit is Drunk for the duration of the game.

A Drunk unit receives a -1 bonus to Resolve and a -1 bonus to its Fight Skill value. A Drunk unit also has a +1 penalty to its Shoot Skill value, all Saves, and every other Test made with that unit.

◊ FORTIFICATIONS

If Fortifications are being used in a scenario, only the defending force has the option to take them. They are purchased with points, just like ships and units.

They are placed in the defender's deployment zone during or right after the terrain is set up on the board. Players may have to compromise on placement and/or deployment a little so Fortifications can be useful to the defender.

A defender's options for Fortifications are the following:

Breastwork: 1 point each

» This is a section of wall or earthworks terrain about 3" to 5" long that provides Hard Cover to models. They may be placed individually, or in a connected fashion.

» Breastwork does not count as a Structure; it is considered object terrain.

Gun Emplacement: 2 points each

» This is an open-topped, single-section mounded earth structure that's about 3" across.

» It has a Fortitude of 5 and an Integrity of 4.

» It may accommodate a Light or Medium Cannon on a naval carriage (not a field carriage). The gun must be purchased separately, and follows the rules (point cost, firing arc, etc.) for Cannons in a Fortification, not on a field carriage *(See Artillery for details p. 72).*

Watchtower: 2 points each

» This is a roofed timber structure with a single section and access points on all 4 sides.

» Its floor is 3" above ground height, and can accommodate only 6 models.

» A Tower's Fortitude and Integrity is 2.

» A Watchtower may mount 1 Swivel Gun, which must be purchased separately.

» This has the Low Profile trait, so Artillery receives a +4 penalty when trying to hit it with a Ranged Attack.

A defender may not take more Fortifications than the number of units in their force.

Though limited for now, the list of available Fortifications will be expanded in a future supplement to *Blood & Plunder.*

◊ HIDDEN SETUP

If a scenario calls for a hidden setup, players assign a number to each unit in their force. Players then take a set of markers with the corresponding numbers on one side, along with two that are blank. If players don't have numbered markers, scraps of paper with numbers written on them work as well.

The defending player first places a marker face down to represent a unit that will deploy in that location, following all pertinent scenario rules. The attacking player does the same. This alternates back and forth until both players run out of markers. The blank markers are placed as well (in order to mislead an opponent).

When all markers have been placed, they are revealed, and the number of the corresponding unit replaces the numbered marker at its location on the board. All units must have at least one model within 1" of the marker and must be Cohesive. Blank markers are removed from the board.

After all units have been placed, play proceeds as normal.

◊ LAY IN WAIT

This Scenario rule represents units that have crept in to an area ahead of the main force, and have kept their whereabouts a secret until the start of the battle. Typically, units with the Elusive, Skirmishers, or Scouts Special Rules can Lay in Wait.

Units that Lay in Wait may set up last, after all other units have been placed on the board. They must be set up in or behind Cover, and must start the battle Prone. They may ignore the scenario rules for deployment and be placed anywhere on the board, but may not be placed within 9" of an enemy unit.

Mounted units and artillery units may not Lay in Wait.

If a unit is set up using this rule and is armed with Matchlock weapons or Torches, it must take a Dedicated action to light the match cords or Torches before using them.

If there is a situation where both attacking and defending players have units that can Lay in Wait, the defending player sets up his units before the attacker.

◊ LIMITED VISIBILITY

Limited Visibility represents conditions where visibility is poor (e.g. fog, smoke, or darkness). This rule can also be applied to areas of terrain (e.g. planted fields and forested areas) if the players wish, and is explained fully in the Terrain section *(p. 64).*

Players assign a range value to the visibility conditions in inches. The harder it is to see, the lower the number. Below are some common visibility ranges:

Night: 12"

Light Rain: 28"

Heavy Rain: 20"

Downpour: 12"

The visibility range is how far a unit can "see" in the given condition. Units within the visibility range can be seen by other units, and are in Cover. Units beyond the visibility range are out of Line of Sight.

If a situation arises where there are two visibility values

(such as heavy rain at night), simply use the lower of the two values.

Visibility may change throughout the course of a game, either by Events or by Scenario rules (for example, a change in the Weather).

Sunrise/Sunset

Visibility can change quickly when the sun is rising or setting.

If this battle is taking place at night, add +4" to the visibility range at the start of the next turn, and at the start of every turn after that until the visibility is 36", in which case the sun has risen and visibility is no longer limited.

If this battle is taking place during the day, the visibility is limited to 36" at the start of the next turn. Subtract -4" to the visibility range at the start of every turn after that until the visibility is 12", in which case the sun has set and visibility is fully limited. Any sun-or-heat-related Weather events are dispelled once the sun begins to set.

Fog

If both players agree, Fog may be chosen as a Limited Visibility condition in effect at the beginning of the battle. Typically, a scenario will start with Heavy Fog, but players may choose Light or Dense Fog instead if both agree.

> **Light Fog:** 16"
>
> **Heavy Fog:** 12"
>
> **Dense Fog:** 8"

Fog density changes and limits Weather events (see Events) in the following ways:

> » If a Weather event is rolled during Fog, the Weather event does not occur. Instead, a negative result on the Weather table causes the fog to become one step less dense, and a positive result makes the fog one step denser.

> » If a negative result is rolled during Light Fog, the Fog lifts. Weather effects can then occur normally, and visibility is no longer limited by Fog.

> » If a positive result is rolled during Dense Fog, nothing happens (Dense Fog is the lowest visibility possible)

Wind direction events have no effect on Fog.

Wind speed Events do effect Fog

> » A wind speed increase (sustained or a Gust) decreases Fog density by one step, and will dispel Light Fog like a negative Weather result (see above).

> » A wind speed decrease (sustained or a Lull) increases Fog density by one step, with Dense fog as the lowest

limit.

Visibility of Structures

Structures are large, and easier to see that units in low visibility conditions. As such, the range to see a Structure is doubled. For example, a unit could see a ship that is 24" away at night, instead of 12".

If a structure has the Low Profile trait, it can only be seen at the normal range given the conditions, not double.

Fires

A burning Structure section will make all units within 6" of it visible from any distance in a scenario that takes place at night. It has no effect on visibility in rain or fog.

◊ LONG RANGE BOMBARDMENT

This rule represents forces with Artillery that are firing on the enemy at long range as they advance. This rarely destroys a target, but may damage it before the battle begins.

Only Structures (including ships) may be the target of a bombardment.

Players decide how many salvos will be fired at long range before a battle begins, and is usually limited by visibility. For example, forces engaging at night may only roll for one bombardment, to reflect the difficult nature of hitting a target in the dark.

We suggest that no more than 3 salvos are rolled before the beginning of a battle.

To roll a salvo:

> » Each player rolls 1 d10 for each Medium Cannon in their force

> » Each player rolls 2 d10 for each Heavy Cannon in their force

> » All dice can be rolled at the same time

A hit is scored on each natural 10. No additional dice are rolled for extra hits, and no Critical Damage is caused by Long Range Bombardment.

Any hits are assigned by the attacking player, but no Structure section can be hit more than once during a salvo, unless all Structure sections have already been hit once. Additionally, the first hit from a salvo that is applied to a ship must be applied to the ships Rigging.

Casualties may be caused by a salvo, as is usual for units in Structure sections that are hit by Artillery. Roll Ranged Saves and remove any Casualties as normal, but the affected unit does not take Fatigue Tests or gain any Fatigue points as a result.

All Artillery used in the bombardment are considered to be reloaded and ready to fire at the start of the battle.

Cannons that can only fire Grapeshot may not be used in a Long Range Bombardment.

◊ RANDOM GAME LENGTH

This rules represents uncertainty of time on the battlefield, be it the onset of bad weather, the arrival of overwhelming reinforcements, or a force running low on ammunition.

A game with random length lasts a minimum of 3 turns. At the end of the third turn, roll a d10 to see if the game continues (see the chart below). If it does, roll at the end of every subsequent turn until a roll is failed. When a roll is failed, the game immediately ends, and victory conditions are determined at that point.

	Turn 4	Turn 5	Turn 6	Turn 7	Turn 8+
Roll needed to start the turn	2+	4+	6+	8+	10

◊ RESERVES

Units held in Reserve do not start on the board at the beginning of battle. This represents units being held as reinforcements, or units that were not fully prepared for the battle at its onset.

If a force has units in Reserve, roll a d10 for each unit in reserve at the start of the second turn. (see chart below). If they do not deploy on the second turn, roll at the beginning of each subsequent turn until they do.

	Turn 2	Turn 3	Turn 4
Roll needed to deploy unit in reserve	6+	4+	Automatic success

Deployed Reserves move onto the board in their force's deployment zone with a Move action, unless a Scenario dictates otherwise. Units must deploy the turn for which they make a successful roll.

If a ship is being held in Reserve, just roll once for the ship. All units aboard the ship arrive with it.

13
Reference Section

13.1 *Ship Stat Summary*

TYPE	SLOOP	BRIGANTINE	LIGHT FRIGATE	LONGBOAT
Point cost	14	16	21	3
Top Speed	4"	4"	5"	4"
Windward	-0"	-1"	-2"	-1"
Turn	4"	3"	3"	3"
Draft	4	6	8	-
Size (Decks)	2	3	3	1
Cannons (Fore/Mid/Aft Deck)	6 (6/-/0)	8 (0/4/4)	14 (2/6/6*)	0
Swivels (Fore/Mid/Aft Deck)	6 (2/-/4)	6 (4/0/2)	4 (2/0/2)	1
Hull Fortitude	4	4	5	2
Hull Integrity	5	6	6	3
Rigging Fortitude	3	3	3	-
Rigging Integrity	4	5	6	-
Sail Settings	4"/2"/0"/A	4"/3"/2"/0"/A	5"/4"/3"/2"/0"/A	3"/0"/A
Traits	Sweeps:2 Simple Rig Fore-and-Aft Rig	Sweeps 2 Stay Sails Hybrid Rig	Stay Sails Chasers: 2 (stern)	Sweeps:4 Low Profile

* Two of the gun ports are "chasers" that face straight backward from the stern of the ship (see below).

13.2 *Ship Traits*

SWEEPS: X: May move up to X" under oars while sails are set at speed 0" and the Sweeps are crewed.

STAYSAILS: When moving under sail to windward, this ship is never reduced to less than its slowest Sail Setting value (unless it is In the Wind's Eye). Use of Staysails is optional.

CHASERS: Chasers are Cannons that face either forward out of the bow, or out back from the stern of the ship. If Cannons are placed in the Chasers gun ports, they may fire in the direction they face, with the width of the bow (or stern) as their Arc of Fire.

FORE-AND-AFT RIG: When this ship attempts a Tacking Advanced Maneuver, it may roll two d10 for the Test, and use the best result. This ship cannot perform the Box Hauling Advanced Maneuver.

HYBRID RIG: As long as this ship's sails are not at their highest setting, it gains the Fore-and-Aft Rig ship trait.

SIMPLE RIG: This ships Sail Setting may be changed using a Standard action instead of a Dedicated action. Additionally, apply a +1 penalty when taking a Shoot Test to hit this ship's Rigging.

LOW PROFILE: Apply a +4 penalty to a Shoot Test attempting to hit the Hull of this ship.

Strike Points and Strike Tests

A force will gain a Strike Point when (if at the end of a turn):

The force has lost 25 percent of its staring models as casualties (one Strike Point for each 25 percent).

One of the force's ships suffers a Catastrophic Damage or Critical Damage result.

A deck on a force's flagship is currently occupied by at least 1 enemy unit. (The flagship is the one that the commander starts the battle on).

- » The Fortitude value of the Hull or Rigging of the force's flagship has been reduced to half its starting value (rounded down).
- » One of the force's ships (not boats) has been immobilized by Critical Damage or Running Aground.
- » One of the force's ships (not boats) has been lost (by capture, fire, or sinking).
- » The enemy force fulfills an objective requirement for the Scenario being played.

Strike Points are cumulative.

If any force has two more Strike Points than the opposing force at the end of a turn, that player's force must immediately roll a Strike Test. Roll one d10, with the Resolve of the force's commander as the target number. If successful, the game moves on to the next turn. Otherwise, the force surrenders and the opponent claims victory!

If a force's commander has been removed as a Casualty, the force automatically fails any Strike Test it may have to make.

13.3 *Critical Damage Tables*

BUILDING CRITICAL DAMAGE

10: TOTAL COLLAPSE

The entire building falls apart and becomes an Area of impassable terrain that blocks Line of Sight. All models within the building are removed as Casualties.

8–9: FIRE

The section targeted by the attack catches fire. Place a Fire marker on the section

Any unit that enters or begins an activation in a burning section must make a Resolve Test with one d10. A failed test causes the unit to gain a point of Fatigue. Units in a burning section may not make any Ranged Attacks.

A successful Repair action made by a unit in a burning section extinguishes the fire in that section and removes the marker.

At the end of the turn, roll a d10. On a 7+, the fire spreads. A section that is not burning but is adjacent to a section with a Fire marker on it is chosen at random, and a Fire marker is placed on it. A fire will not spread from a section if that Fire marker was placed there late in the turn, and the structure owner didn't have any units left to activate to try to put out the fire.

A structure may not have more than one Fire marker on each section. If a section were to gain a second fire marker, the structure is destroyed (*see Total Collapse above*).

2–7: DEBRIS

One model in the struck section is immediately removed without a Save (defending player's choice). If there are no models in the struck section, treat this as No Effect.

1 OR LESS: NO EFFECT

FORTIFICATION CRITICAL DAMAGE

10: BREACH

Place a 4" breach marker anywhere along the section targeted by the Artillery. This 3" area of scattered rubble is considered to provide Hard Cover and slows movement by -1" per Move Action. The breach also leads to the Fortification's interior (the area or section directly behind the breach). If any models are within that section, d5 of them take hits (Ranged Saves are allowed).

9: FIRE

The section targeted by the attack catches fire. Place a Fire marker on the section

Any unit that enters or begins an activation in a burning section must make a Resolve Test with one d10. A failed test causes the unit to gain a point of Fatigue. Units in a burning section may not make any Ranged Attacks.

A successful Repair action made by a unit in a burning section extinguishes the fire in that section and removes the marker.

At the end of the turn, roll a d10. On a 7+, the fire spreads. A section that is not burning but is adjacent to a section with a Fire marker on it is chosen at random, and a Fire marker is placed on it. A fire will not spread from a section if that Fire marker was placed there late in the turn, and the structure owner didn't have any units left to activate to try to put out the fire.

A structure may not have more than one Fire marker one each section. If a section were to gain a second fire marker, the structure is destroyed (all models are removed as Casualties, and the structure becomes an area of impassable terrain that blocks Line of Sight).

6–8: GUN DESTROYED

An Artillery piece is chosen and removed from the struck section by the player controlling the Fortification. It must be a gun within the attacker's Arc of Fire, and must be one facing the attacker, if possible. If not, remove a different gun.

If no gun can be removed, remove a model in the line of fire as a casualty (without a Save) instead. If there are no models to remove, treat it as No Effect.

2–5: DEBRIS

One model in the struck section is immediately removed without a Save (defending player's choice). If there are no models in the struck section, treat this as No Effect.

1 OR LESS: NO EFFECT

SHIP HULL CRITICAL DAMAGE

Ships with 1 section (Boats) have a simplified Critical Damage table due to their small size and simple construction. That table is found below.

10: CATASTROPHIC DAMAGE

The ship shudders and threatens to fall apart. The force associated with the ship gains a Strike Point at the end of this turn. (Strike Points and Strike Tests are explained in the Scenarios section *p.133*.)

The ship gains a Leak marker (*see below*), and then the player rolls again on this table, and applies a second critical damage result. If the second result is a 10, the powder magazine of the ship explodes. Remove the ship from the board, and remove all units on it as Casualties.

Any other Structure section that is touching the ship when it explodes (like a dock or the deck of a grappled ship) will catch fire on a d10 roll of 8+. See the Fire Critical Damage result below.

9: FIRE

The deck targeted by the attack catches fire. Place a Fire marker on the deck, or an adjacent deck if the targeted deck already has one.

Any unit that enters or begins an Activation on a burning deck must make a Resolve Test with one d10. A failed test causes the unit to gain a point of Fatigue. Units on a burning deck may not make any Ranged Attacks.

A successful Repair action made by a unit on a burning deck extinguishes the fire in that section and removes the marker.

At the end of the turn, roll a d10. On a 7+, the fire spreads. The ship owner chooses a deck that is not already on fire, and places a Fire marker on the newly burning deck. A fire will not spread from a section if that Fire marker was placed there late in the turn, and the ship owner didn't have any units left to activate to try to put out the fire.

A ship may not have more than one Fire marker on each deck. If a deck were to gain a second fire marker because all decks are burning, the ship is Destroyed.

A fire can spread to a ship that is fouled with (*see Collisions p. 87*) or connected via grapples to a burning ship, but only when the original ship has fire markers on all of its decks.

8: STEERAGE

The ship's steering is damaged. Add a Damage marker to the ships Steerage.

If the Steerage has one Damage marker, the ship's turn value is reduced by half (rounded down).

If the Steerage has two Damage markers, the ship no longer moves under sail normally. It will instead drift 3" or at its current Sail Setting when it moves, whichever is less.

If the ship already has two Damage markers on the Steer-

age, no more markers can be added, and the Hull of the ship takes an additional point of Damage instead.

One steerage Damage marker can be removed by each successful Repair action.

6–7 GUN

An Artillery piece is chosen and removed from the struck deck section by the player controlling the Ship. It must be a gun within the attacker's Arc of Fire, and must be one facing the attacker, if possible. If this is not possible, remove a different gun.

If no gun can be removed, the ship's hull receives an additional point of damage) instead.

4–5: LEAK

The deck targeted by the attack suffers a major leak. Place a Leak marker on that deck targeted, or an adjacent deck if the targeted deck already has one.

Leak markers do not have any effect on units.

A successful Repair action made by a unit on a leaking deck repairs the Leak in that section and removes the marker.

At the end of the turn, roll a d10 only if no attempt was made to repair the Leak that turn. On a 7+, the ship takes on water. The ship owner chooses a deck that is not already leaking, and places a Leak marker on the new deck. A ship will not take on water if that Leak marker was placed there late in the turn, and the ship owner didn't have any units left to activate to try to fix the leak.

A ship may never have more than one Leak marker per section. If a ship were to ever be forced to take more than 1 Leak marker on a section because all sections have Leak markers, the ship starts to sink. (*See Sinking Ships below.*)

◊ SINKING SHIPS

When a ship (not a boat) starts to sink, it is destroyed at the end of the next full turn. During the time while the ship is sinking, units on the ship may take actions as normal to try to escape, but may not attempt any Ranged Attacks.

A sinking ship cannot be sailed or rowed, and can only drift (unless it was Anchored).

A ship that has Run Aground does not sink, but the same rules apply. (The ship slowly breaks apart while being battered by wind and sea.)

When a ship sinks at the end of the turn, the ship is removed from the board and all units still onboard are removed as Casualties.

Any units on the sinking ship that are engaged in a Melee Combat with another ship are not removed as Casualties when the ship sinks, but if they become Shaken in the course of that Melee Combat , they automatically Rout. (In essence, they are clinging to the rail of the enemy ship as theirs goes under!)

2–3: RIGGING CRITICAL HIT.

Roll once on the Ship Rigging Critical Damage table. Apply any effects to the mast on the targeted deck. If the deck section does not contain a mast, the Hull takes an additional point of damage instead.

1 OR LESS: NO EFFECT

SHIP RIGGING CRITICAL DAMAGE

10: MAST DESTROYED

One of the ship's masts is shattered and falls into the water, impeding ship movement until the lines are cut away.

Place a Mast Destroyed marker on the deck containing the targeted mast. As long as that marker is there, the ship is immobilized and can only drift (unless Anchored or Run Aground).

The Mast Destroyed marker can be removed by a successful Repair action taken by a unit on the affected deck.

When the marker is removed, the ship immediately loses its highest Sail Setting. This effect is cumulative If multiple masts are lost. If a ship has no masts left, it is immobilized.

7–9: SHEETS & SHROUDS

Some of the ship's control or support lines have been severed. Place a Sheets & Shrouds Damage marker on the ship. Apply a -1 modifier to all Advanced Maneuvers or Sail Settings tests for each of these markers the ship has.

One marker may be removed with each successful Repair action.

1–6: SAIL & SPAR DAMAGE

The ship's sails or spars have taken significant damage. Place a Sail & Spar Damage marker on the ship. The affected ship's current Sail Setting is reduced by 1" for each of these markers the ship has taken. A ship cannot take more Sail & Spar Damage markers than the value of its maximum Sail Setting. (So a ship with a maximum Sail Setting of 5" can't take more than five Sail & Spar Damage marker.)

One marker may be removed with each successful Repair action.

0 OR LESS: NO EFFECT

BOAT CRITICAL DAMAGE

10: DESTROYED

The boat suffers catastrophic damage. It falls apart and sinks to the bottom of the sea. The ship is removed from the board and all units on board are removed as Casualties.

6–9: RIGGING DESTROYED

The boat's rigging is ripped away. The boat may not move under sail for the rest of the battle.

If the boat does not have Rigging, or it has already been lost, this result does an additional point of damage to the Hull instead.

2–5: LEAK

The boat suffers a major leak. Place a Leak marker on the boat.

Leak markers do not have any negative effect on units.

A successful Repair action made by a unit on a leaking boat repairs the Leak and removes the marker.

At the end of the turn, roll a d10 only if no attempt was made to repair the leak that turn. On a 7+, the ship takes on water and sinks. A ship will not take on water if that Leak marker was placed there late in the turn, and the ship owner didn't have any units left to activate to try to fix the leak.

If the boat has a Leak marker, and it is forced to take another Leak marker for any reason, it immediately sinks.

If the boat sinks, remove the boat from the board, and all units in the boat are removed as Casualties.

1 OR LESS: NO EFFECT

13.4 *Templates and Counters*

You may reproduce these pages to cut out the templates for use in your games of Blood & Plunder

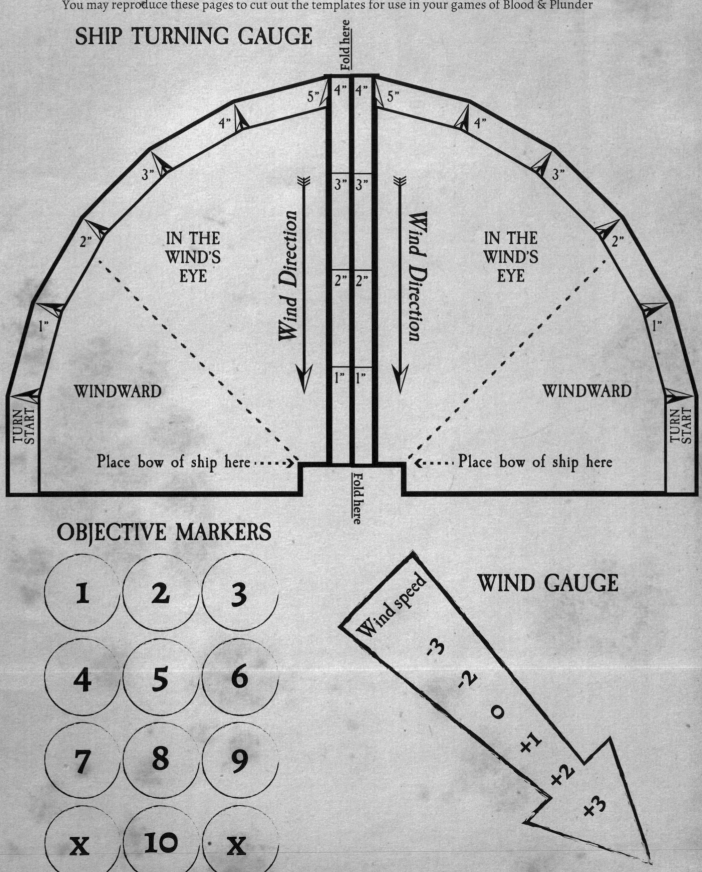

SHIP TURNING GAUGE

Fold here

5" 4" 4" 5"

4" 4"

3"

Wind Direction

3" 3"

Wind Direction

3"

2"

IN THE WIND'S EYE

2" 2"

IN THE WIND'S EYE

2"

1"

1" 1"

1"

WINDWARD

WINDWARD

TURN START

Place bow of ship here ·····▸

◂····· Place bow of ship here

TURN START

Fold here

OBJECTIVE MARKERS

(1) (2) (3)

(4) (5) (6)

(7) (8) (9)

(X) (10) (X)

WIND GAUGE

Wind speed

-3 -2 0 +1 +2 +3

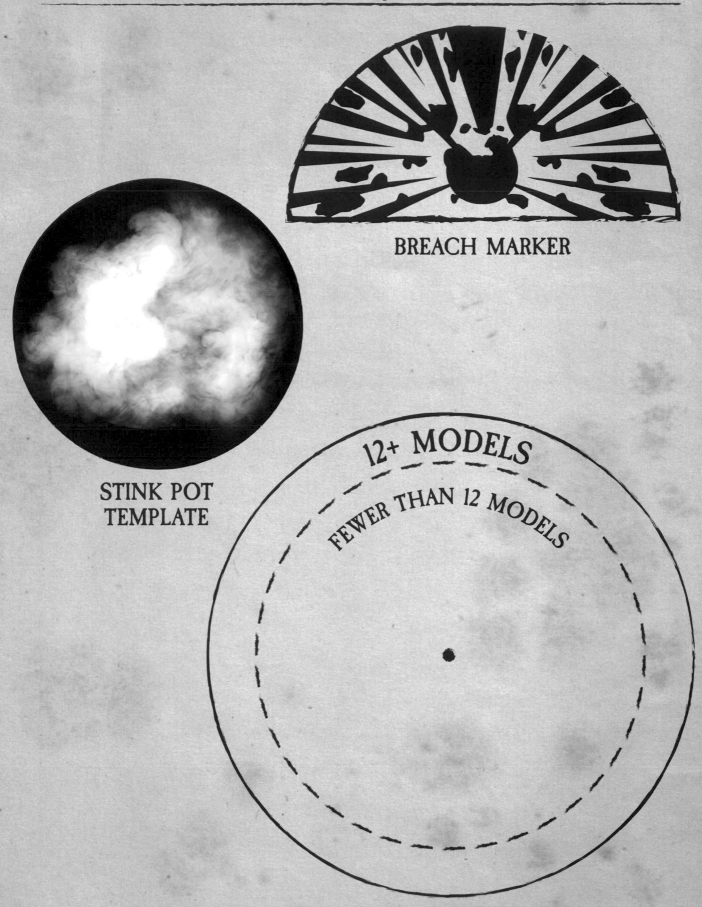

BREACH MARKER

STINK POT
TEMPLATE

12+ MODELS

FEWER THAN 12 MODELS

COHESION TEMPLATE

Come Build Your Crew at
FIRELOCKGAMES.COM

THANK YOU TO ALL OUR BACKERS

Matthew S. Robertson
Heath Thompson
Brendan Zandi
Stephen Stanton
Lee Wendel
Chris Wiesland
Joe Vespaziani
Alan Skinner
Douglas Wildfong
Colin Ashton
William Haeussler
Krishna Lonkani
Robert Tankersley
Samantha Clayton
Sergio Robaina
Matthew Schleis
Steve Mccuen
Jim Kares
David Wolf
Ronald Loosvelt
Shay Wallace
Michael Ferkin
Steve Hill
George S Rizzo
Carlos Langa Morales
Michael Edelstein
Timothy Wright
Mark Tarver
Oscar Quintana
Edouard Foraz
Timothy Roller
David Royer
Tracy Vierra
Gus Hammer
Thomas A. Hoff
David Dujordan
Trevor Fetherstonhaugh
Johnathan Ho
Nick Cook
Joe Clark
Liam Taylor
Mark Van Der Upwich
Benjamin Scherer
Karsten Keese
Ian Jackson
Reg Newell
Roland Hilgarth
Marcus Folz
Kevin Schwarz
Clayton Bannister
Brad Ballard
Yuri Devilbiss
Thomas H Zelewske
Darren Byers
Neil Mancer
Victor Pérez Cazorla
Jonathan Gray
Anthony Cassano
Kroum Batchvarov
Rohan Dwyer
Matthew Cwick
Bruce A. Euans
John Lamulle
Russell Helms
Frederique Josseaume
Paul Flebus
Jeremey M. Davis
Lee Moran
Fredrick Barbee
Christopher Pinder
Eric Sharrer
Todd Kinkade
Jon Finn
Erick Moreno
Winston
Kevin M Hamrick
Stewart Weir
Paul Dempsey
Josh
Douglas Craig
Rune Hoff Lauridsen

Terrell Scoggins
Tom Mills
Hector Penton
Brent Sinclair
Andrew Spong
Sam Newell
Nate Zettle
Michael Gellar
Oscar "Peg Boy" Morejon
Chris Welsh
Nicholas Taylor
Shawn Bulger
Jon Van Geest
Craig Henderson
Timothy Hough
Edward Regendahl
Dave Mitchell
Raymond Wiggins
Peter Webb
Matthew Thorenz
Ohad Kanne
Scott Howland
Robbie J Rauch
Sean Martin
Eric Sarlin
Melanie Wilkins
Joshua Sprague
Alan Shirey
Richard Demorris
Unai Mujika
Jeremy Hendrix
Michael Overstreet
Frank Azor
Jason Kimbro
Tom Pace
Roger Berry
Matt Gregory
Matt Hurdle
Anthony Dalo
Clayton Flint
Claus Paludan
Isaiah Mitchell
Adam Solis
Joshua Mcgary
Jeremy Spurlock
Jordan Agudelo
Dwaine Balius
Henny Dings
Timothy Griffin
Kevin Shope
Jonathan W Rusten
Jordan Fox
Tht
Marcus Hatchell
Jake Rose
Andreas Valder
John
Ulrich Drees
Peter Palmer
Mark G Lawrence
Matt Saia
Paul Smith
Charlie St Clair
Ewan Farish
Martin Leventon
George Panopoulos
Ross Hutchins
Keith Hooper
Darren Gourley
Sora
Anthony Garland
Ray Guerrero
James Killen
Carlos Salvador
William Gaskins
Ben Lockard
Christopher Camacho
Dylan Bright
Todd Rigertas
Konstantin Dika
Joseph Fusco

Greg Whitaker
Black Knight Games
Christian Schmal
Chris Bennett
Christopher J Kenna
Regino Sanchez
David Blair
Dave Ring
Mike Hart
Gustavo Barona
Jonathan Buchanan
Eric Staeheli
Tod Sistrunk
Ol' Billy Riley Blair
Hamish Cooper
Jordi Salvador Bernadí
Shaun Allen
Daniel Gaghan
Brian Schoner
Adam
Matthew K Green
José Ignacio Macaya Sanz
Joel Hall
James Beattie
Henrik Dahl Jensen
Frank Blau
Peter Baldwin
Dirk Ipendahl
Per-Olov Gothe
Francesco Caruso
Patrick Ballinger
David Fairhurst
Jonathan Jones
Claus Appel
John Munro
Cyrus Lendvay
Duane Boyd
William Warren
Andrew Kweik
Dean Broadway
Jesper Asmussen
Paul Hickling
Pereira José
Carmen J Viola
Chollet
Joshua T Hart
Bradley Schweitzer
Michael S Bagley
Chris Tate
Anthony Silvey
Jonas Petersson
Kevin Taylor
Tracy Vorisek
Frank Clark (Care Of Ecolin)
Nicholas Hendley
Don Fritz
Mark Chapman
Nathan Hanes
Patrick Chartrand-Chamblay
Brian R Babcock
Richard Campbell
Ian Beal
Ian Baldwin
Dominic Rapini
Courtney Little
Jose Vasquez
Steven Baxter
Barry Keight
Oliver Haywood
Ben Williams
Vytas Masteika
Bruce Harlick
Michael
Steven Carroll
Sam Linde
Byron Bornhorst
Sean Swift
Nick Bailey
Eric Walker
Gerry Cupp
Jim Autry

Graeme Rigg
Martin Gallo
Timothy Carroll
David Cook
Ian Manson
Cameron Smith
Stuart Macpherson
Charles Scott Christian
Paul N. Thornton
Damien Hansen
Paul Dejardin
Ron Hathaway
Scott Glitz
Robert Hoppenrath
Bruce Heasman
Ralph Mazza
Ernest Reimer
Christopher Flint
Mr C Charlton
Captain Steven Soler
Alistair Cleave
Daniel Ottalini
Ian Nash
Thomas Zelewske
Dave Walker
Anthony Selley
Alex Colbert
Matt Finn
Michael Weaver
Michael Corton
Paul Meyer
Mike Whitaker
Shaun King
James Maclennan
Michael Westenhouser
Robert Strawder
Matt Barker
Michael Halstead
Vincent Rospond
Dylan Asmus
Mike Sterling
David Hunter
Kevin Abramow
Brian Horton
Dan Baker
Robert Seitz
Kevin Cook
Armen Aslanian
Sauron
Scott Alex
Jonathan Ow
John Sweet
Chris Bloch
Stuart Morell
Ray Op'tland
David Boyle
Paul Coates
Wayne Burton
Alan Dearn
Gabriel Moss
William Case
Jason Riffle
Ronald James
Gates Imbeau
Alan Chenery
Lorne Clarke
Christopher Smallwood
Mike Rhoda
Belle Litton-Bunag
Ron Carnegie
Kevin Carroll
Jerry Lane
Thomas G. Maybin
Brandon Sivret
Alex C. Smith
Blake Shrode
Damon Richardson
Dan Helmen
Alfred Kirkham
Bruce Clegg
Michael Dunsmore

David Manley
Robert Ackling
Alvaro Montes Bermejo
Todd C Lowman
Urban Blom
Graham Robinson
John Montrie
Andrew Bouffard
Richard Bisso
Tim Bentley
Mr John Dale
Murray Brewer
Garry Sharp
Lee W Wood
David Brittain
Tristan Cotterill
Benjamin Martin
Alex Robinson
James Sherriff
Mr D A Robertson
Darren Miller
Théodore Georgescou
Martin Noel
Henning Peters
Matt Strange
Richard Sherpherd
Isabel Collier
Andrei Novac
Stephen Keating
Jussi-Pekka Korpela
Wesley Kennedy
Brian Shope
John Larson
Jan Zimmermann
Charles Dirk Flaherty
Ian White
Josh Peery
Christian Mejstrik
Jeff Lawrence
Steven Buerkle
John Bornmann
Matt Helmen
Bing Sarum Feng
Javier Pio Gutierrez
Bryce Pearcy
Steve Large
John Burkwall
Deborah Malamud
Tym Corbett
Sean Kelly
Blain Smith
Jack Van Niekerk
Sean Kahlich
Anthony Bonifonte
Malcolm Tuck
David F Donovan
Dale Wentz
Peter Hickson
Alex Netten
David Loyd-Hearn
Keith Jenkins
Christopher Pawley
Scott Stewart
Benjamin Nicholls
Richard Newman
Douglas Hamilton
Bradley Cobden
Richard Malpas
Kristopher Mischloney
Matthew Shelander
Clint Williams
Jacob Gilbar
Richard Rush
Scott Cunningham
Carl Rosa
Mark Meyer
Duncan Parton
Christian Sørup Jensen
Jason Wagoner
Joachim Deckart
Jonathan Dispigno

Mark Somogyi
Daniel Desmarais
Chris Kirby
Chris Fernandez
Axel Demenet
Joonas Joensuu
Dana Napier
Paul Harris
Andy Freeman
Colin Matthews
Jeremy Bailey
Guillaume Roy
Dan Mazur
Nicholas Longtin
Erik G Tausendfreund
Daniel Rees
Troy Wold
Roy Smallpage
Sean Kotch
Gregg Radtke
Carsten Woitas
Charles Tornow
John Bays
Denis Vermeyen
Enrique Durand
John Dehart
Paul Wind
John Mackrory
Henrik Wikman
James A Peterson Jr
Mikki R Brack
Gerrit L Swaneveld
J. Scott Cunningham
Michael Lombardi
Steven Alban
Scott Laskey
Paul Wood
Patrick Boudet
Kieran Mcgrann
Mick Rood
Huron Romaric
Andreas Persson
Justin Atwell
Michael Rinaldi
Robert Wilson
Neil Amswych
Chris Ward
Christian Classen
Max Nelson
Jeff Olsen
Jorel Miller
Raul A Jimenez
Richard Smith
Daniel Mynett
Michael Petrochilos
R. Codey Morton
Robert Coleman
Brandon Ames
Jesus Segundo Ariza
Todd Lloyd
Thomas Meredith
Ben Robinson
Yair Robinson
Bryan Rawls
Peter M Hope
Mark Buffington
Geoff Golliver
John Baldwin
Jordan Marvel
Brian Wilk
Caesar Barillas
Ronny Heinz
Christian Templin
David Niblock
Seb Mullins
Lefort Emmanuel
Brian L. Bird
Daniel Angelino
Jim Johnson
Stefan Sheckells
Joseph Trybus